TIM STAFFORD

SEXUAL CHAOS

Charting a
Course Through
Turbulent Times

INTERVARSITY PRESS
DOWNERS GROVE, ILLINOIS 60515
LEICESTER, ENGLAND

InterVarsity Press

P.O. Box 1400, Downers Grove, Illinois 60515, USA
38 De Montfort Street, Leicester LE1 7GP, England

©1989 by Christianity Today, Inc.

Revised edition ©1993 by Tim Stafford

First edition published under the title The Sexual Christian.

All rights reserved. No part of this publication may be reproduced, stored in a retrieval system, or transmitted, in any form or by any means, electronic, mechanical, photocopying, recording or otherwise, without the prior permission of InterVarsity Press.

InterVarsity Press, U.S.A., is the book-publishing division of InterVarsity Christian Fellowship, a student movement active on campus at hundreds of universities, colleges and schools of nursing in the United States of America, and a member movement of the International Fellowship of Evangelical Students. For information about local and regional activities, write Public Relations Dept., InterVarsity Christian Fellowship, 6400 Schroeder Rd., P.O. Box 7895, Madison, WI 53707-7895.

Inter-Varsity Press, England, is the book-publishing division of the Universities and Colleges Christian Fellowship (formerly the Inter-Varsity Fellowship), a student movement linking Christian Unions in universities and colleges throughout the United Kingdom and the Republic of Ireland, and a member movement of the International Fellowship of Evangelical Students. For information about local and national activities in Great Britain write to UCCF, 38 De Montfort Street, Leicester LE1 7GP.

All Scripture quotations, unless otherwise indicated, are taken from the North American edition of the HOLY BIBLE, NEW INTERNATIONAL VERSION®. NIV®. Copyright ©1973, 1978, 1984 by International Bible Society. Used by permission of Zondervan Publishing House. British edition published by Hodder and Stoughton Ltd. All rights reserved.

USA ISBN 0-8308-1349-7
UK ISBN 0-85110-991-8

Printed in the United States of America

Library of Congress Cataloging-in-Publication Data

Stafford, Tim.
    Sexual chaos: charting a course through turbulent times/
    Tim Stafford.
       p.   cm.
    Includes bibliographical references.
    ISBN 0-8308-1349-7
    1. Sex—Religious aspects—Christianity.   2. Marriage—Religious
aspects—Christianity.   3. Sex role—Religious aspects—
Christianity.   I. Title.
BT708.S79   1993
241'.66—dc20   *93-19209*
                                                          CIP

British Library Cataloguing in Publication Data

A catalogue record for this book is available from the British Library.

17	16	15	14	13	12	11	10	9	8	7	6	5	4	3	2	1
07	06	05	04	03	02	01	00	99	98	97	96	95	94	93		

Acknowledgments

This book is largely taken from *The Sexual Christian,* part of a series published by Christianity Today Inc. I am able to expand and develop it for a wider audience thanks to the generosity of Harold Myra and Paul Robbins, leaders at CTi. They are good friends, to whom I am indebted in many ways.

I want particularly to thank my brother, William Stafford, for sharing his insights and historical knowledge. He answered many questions and let me read some of his work in progress. He, Philip Yancey and my editor Rodney Clapp helped enormously with the shape as well as the content of the book. It is a joy to have such friends and colleagues.

Finally, I want to acknowledge the support and love of my wife, Popie, without whom this book would not be possible, in more ways than one.

1
SEXUAL CHAOS

B lond, blue-eyed Trever Fudger was just nine months old when his grandmother, Ruth Ann Bergstrom, called 911 to report a medical emergency. Paramedics raced to the Bergstrom home in quiet, rural Sebastopol, California. They could have taken their time. When they arrived Trever was dead, long dead. His torso was mottled with deep purple bruises. Rigor mortis had already set in his tiny body.

An autopsy revealed that Trever had been struck or kicked repeatedly. Internal injuries included broken ribs and a torn liver. His forty-year-old grandmother and her thirty-year-old husband, Christopher Bergstrom, were charged with his death, and subsequently pleaded guilty.

The Santa Rosa *Press Democrat* (December 13, 1992, p. A1) reported that Trever's mother, a nineteen-year-old high-school dropout named

Shannon Grimes, had left Trever with her mother for the weekend. During the weekend Ruth Ann went out, leaving Christopher to watch the baby. Christopher was watching professional wrestling on TV when noise from the baby disturbed and angered him. He allegedly kicked and slugged Trever to stop his crying. He had never liked the child, witnesses said, because he did not get along with the child's father, Shannon Grimes's ex-boyfriend, Kirt Fudger.

When Ruth Ann came home to find the baby injured, her husband suggested taking him to a hospital. She argued him out of it, fearing that authorities would suspect child abuse. After the child had stopped breathing, she and her husband tried to cover up evidence by dressing the baby in the clothes he had originally come in and taking photos of the bruises. They were trying to make it seem as though the child's injuries had occurred before he came for the weekend.

During her mother's trial Shannon Grimes said that she hoped her mother went to prison for just as long as her mother's husband. "Maybe she didn't cause my son to die, but she didn't try to help him."

Who Is Responsible?

Who caused Trever Fudger's death? Christopher Bergstrom did, by punching and kicking a helpless infant. Ruth Ann Bergstrom did, by failing to intervene. Those of us who had no direct involvement in Trever Fudger's death, however, cannot completely absolve ourselves. We are part of a society that produces such cases on a regular basis, due to the sexual chaos we sanction.

At first glance, Trever Fudger's death seems to have nothing to do with sexuality. Probe deeper, though, and you find familiar symptoms. You can almost see the problem in the names the newspaper reported: three different family names in three different generations. Trever's death shows all the usual signs of sexual chaos:

☐ a teenage mother who was herself abused as a child and who had her baby out of wedlock

☐ an absent father

☐ a divorced and remarried grandmother
☐ a stepgrandfather who is thirty years old and is left to care for a baby
he is known to dislike

Trever inherited at least two generations of sexual chaos. He paid for it with his life.

Goodby to the Old Consensus

We are in a sexual transition. The old consensus about how we should live sexually has shattered, and we have not yet arrived at whatever will replace it. We have only arrived at chaos, and with it great pain and confusion. Families shatter. Children grow up with a series of unfamiliar men. They move from home to home, experiencing dizzyingly different levels of poverty and affluence. The old ways of courtship, marriage and family are shaky. For families like Trever Fudger's, they are utterly blown away.

People who grew up before World War II often misunderstand our current sexual situation. They look around and think they see rampant immorality. But if by immorality you mean knowing what is right and deciding not to do it, immorality is not what they see. Immoral lives are what some lived in the Roaring Twenties, flouting convention for the fun of it. Rebellious lives are what a minority lived in the sixties, as they challenged the status quo and claimed to see a new utopia ahead. *Chaotic* lives are more typical today. People don't know what they are supposed to do. They only know that they have powerful urges for love and for sex and for children. They are driven along by forces beyond their understanding. They are making up the rules as they go along, or imitating something they saw on TV.

True, old forms like marriage still remain. But they have grown weak, hollowed out from the inside. They are like European royalty: ceremony and costumes intact, but real power gone. Couples still romp through churches every June, repeating vows, but it is doubtful whether they mean anything very serious by it.

Sexuality is plastic and can be shaped in many different ways, as anthropologists have proved through their research into small, remote tribes with strange (to us) sexual customs. Sexuality is powerful and *must* be shaped, as anthropologists have also proved, for no cultures exist where sexuality has no rules. Civilizations regulate sexuality. Before human beings can paint and sculpt, before they can trade or manufacture, before they can even eke a living from the soil, they must know how to live sexually. Sex is too urgent to leave to guesswork.

Human beings need guidelines for the roles they are expected to play as men and women. They need to know how to bond with the opposite sex. They need to know how to raise and protect children. Fifty years ago, those guidelines were clear to Westerners. Today, they are not.

Trying for Happiness

We didn't go looking for chaos. On the contrary, chaos is the end result of an unprecedented push for pleasure. Americans have never known so much about their sexuality, talked so much about their sexuality or tried so hard for happiness in the sexual realm. Magazines and books and TV talk shows endlessly discuss how to find sexual delight. But the results have been disastrous on every level.

A few years ago Wilt Chamberlain, the great basketball player, published a book in which he claimed to have had sex with twenty thousand women—1.2 a day, he calculated, on average. The sports section of my town's paper printed a column that treated this claim as a huge joke. When I read that ha-ha, boys-will-be-boys response I thought to myself, *I ought to write a note to the sports editor asking whether anybody at the newspaper has been awake during the last ten years. That kind of behavior is not funny anymore.* (It never really was.) I didn't write the letter, and the next day I didn't have to: another great basketball player, Magic Johnson, announced he had the HIV virus. He got it (and gave it, too, quite possibly) behaving in the same merry way Wilt Chamberlain had.

The path that was supposed to provide liberation, joyful sex and self-discovery has led, instead, to death.

Thanks to AIDS, our sexual scene has turned sober. Condoms, which used to be birth control, have become death control. Therapists often treat sexual addiction, a "disease" that would have provoked great hilarity in any male dormitory at my college twenty years ago. But sexual promiscuity is no longer funny or fun.

AIDS has brought terribly serious talk about the courage of its victims, and the compassion they should be shown, and the need to promote "safe" sex. But still hardly anybody raises the possibility that we have a crisis too big for mere courage and compassion and condoms to overcome. It is not merely an AIDS crisis. AIDS is one symptom of a larger crisis. We have a crisis of sexual chaos.

A Health Crisis

Without sexual chaos, AIDS would be merely a clinical curiosity. The disease would be deadly, but isolated to occasional cases or small populations.

AIDS spreads wherever prostitution and promiscuity are rampant, wherever war or materialism or secularism have broken down traditional scruples. In most of the world, AIDS is primarily a heterosexual disease. In the United States AIDS got a head start among gays, but other populations seem to be catching up. For example, nobody knows yet (as I write) whether AIDS is raging through the highly promiscuous teenage population of America, but that possibility increasingly worries epidemiologists. Since the incubation period for AIDS is so long, teenagers who contract the virus while in high school might not know they are infected before they graduate from college. By then they will have had opportunity to infect many others.

Whole populations are at risk, here and around the world. While it is true that other diseases—cancer, heart congestion—kill more, these are not multiplying. We simply do not know how far AIDS will go or how many millions will die from it. The latest World Health Organization estimate is that forty million will be infected by the year 2000.[1] That would be twice the death toll of World War II. But no one really knows.

We do know that AIDS is, in principle, completely preventable. Biology does not give AIDS its power. Sexual chaos does. AIDS spreads wherever sexual chaos has spread.

AIDS is not the only disease warning us about sexual chaos. We have unprecedented levels of less dramatic sexually transmitted diseases, some incurable, some difficult to detect. In addition to the familiar gonorrhea and syphilis—very serious diseases, which are multiplying to remarkable levels and in some cases developing a resistance to antibiotics—we have chlamydia, genital herpes, venereal warts, PID and other diseases a previous generation of doctors never heard of. While none of these diseases is itself fatal if properly treated, they are strongly associated with birth defects, uterine cancer and ectopic pregnancies, which can be fatal. They are also a primary cause of infertility.

Add to these the truly dreadful health problems associated with urban ghettos, where sexual chaos has reached its endpoint. Babies born addicted to crack, babies born prematurely or with disabilities due to malnutrition, women and children who appear in hospital emergency rooms with broken arms or bullet wounds: these also are symptoms of a health crisis that grows from a social crisis.

Gender Confusion
Sexual chaos has brought confusion at every level, starting with the simplest and (seemingly) most innocuous. Once boys and girls grew up knowing that men and women were meant to be attracted together. A little boy knew that he would someday court a girl, even though he believed girls to be yucky. A little girl knew, simply from knowing that she was a girl, that she would someday be courted. Now the mere fact of their gender tells them nothing. According to the current wisdom they may be heterosexual, homosexual or bisexual, meant to live out totally different roles—and there is no test they can take to tell which. For adolescents, at least, this is confusing and frightening. They're told (inaccurately) that one out of ten is a homosexual, so they have to wonder: Am I the one? Is he? Is she?

I will discuss the ethics of homosexuality in a later chapter; my purpose here is to point out how much uncertainty has been introduced.

Even when people are clear on their sexual identity, there's great confusion about how they should express sexual attraction. On the one hand, the media are full of erotic incitements. Every beer ad, every film, stimulates sexual excitement. It's the most natural thing in the world, after sitting through one of these movies, to turn to your partner and imitate what you've seen.

On the other hand, there's tremendous worry over sexual harassment. A man who leers at Madonna's *Sex* is considered normal, but should he leer in the same way at his officemate he could get fired. (Or he could get a date: it's not clear.) Are women sex objects or not? Or is there some way to act that's in between? These are confusing questions for young men, and young women have their own: Should I flirt? Can I encourage a man's advances and then tell him to stop? Is it possible to date a guy and not have sex, or am I in need of therapy if I even think that way?

Confusion continues after people are married. The old patterns of manly providers and feminine nurturers have disintegrated, but nothing has replaced them. When a couple set up house together, they don't have any set role expectations to guide them. Men don't want to act like their fathers—insensitive, unhelping brutes that they were; women don't want to go through what their mothers went through. But apart from the things they want to avoid, and some very general sentiments about freedom and equality, men and women are groping.

In principle men's and women's roles are said to be interchangeable. Women can earn a living, men can clean house. That means that roles must be defined from scratch (and redefined every so often) for every relationship. In practice the roles work out sadly clearer than that: men often impregnate and escape, and women both earn *and* clean house. It's confusing, and often it's painful.

I am not suggesting that the "good old days" were very good. Much needed to change. Unfortunately, we have not changed to a new, better way. We have changed to chaos.

Courtship Confusion

There used to be a well-defined pathway by which two people bonded together in love and formed a family. The old saw summed it up: "First comes love, then comes marriage, then comes Mary with a baby carriage." A young man and a young woman would first date, then go steady, then be engaged, then marry and take on the responsibilities and delights of sexual intimacy, including children. There was a careful progression from uncommitted to committed, from casual friends to intimate lovers to family.

It doesn't work that way anymore. Most people begin sexual intercourse while they are teenagers. Only about a quarter of teenage girls report feeling glad after they lost their virginity (boys are more positive),[2] but once they begin having sex they nearly always continue, not only with their current partner but afterward with other boyfriends or girlfriends. For most, sex becomes a normal part of dating. They meet, they date, they have sex—and then they go their separate ways. Virtually no teenage relationships go on to marriage. Teenagers do go on to other partners. According to the Family Research Council's publication *Free to Be Family,* "Sexually active 18-year-olds today have had on average more sexual partners than the present group of 40-year-old women has had in their entire lives."[3]

They don't stay with their sexual partners, but they do get pregnant. Teenagers should not be parents, nearly everyone agrees. In the United States, billions of dollars have been spent by the government trying, through sex education programs, to keep teenagers from conceiving. These efforts have not succeeded. According to Planned Parenthood's own research, only about a third of sexually active teenagers use birth control consistently, and for those who have had a comprehensive sex education course in school, the percentage rises to a grand 40 percent.[4] That's nowhere close to a passing grade. It's no surprise, then, that one out of ten teenage girls gets pregnant every year.[5] Perhaps a third of all girls become pregnant at least once during their teenage years.[6]

Those who give birth come disproportionately from poor families.

Inevitably their education is disrupted, if not ended. While some studies have suggested that it is possible for these girls to recover, there is no doubt whatsoever that having a baby is a disaster for most teenagers. Indeed, teenagers regard it precisely as that. The vast majority end up raising the child alone, and most of these end up in poverty. (Fifty-three percent of U.S. children living with their mother alone fall below the poverty line, compared to 10 percent of children living with two parents.[7])

For teenagers who choose to have an abortion, the consequences are less tangible. They go quietly about their business, and quite possibly even their parents do not know what has happened. Abortions bring health risks, of course, like all intrusive medical procedures, but their greatest risk is psychological. Abortions cause deep distress. Often the pain comes back full force years later.

Teenage relationships almost never survive a pregnancy. No matter how much the boy swears to stand by the girl, he's nearly always moved on within a short time.[8]

Broken Dreams
Teenagers still have dreams about their wedding and the happy family they will form. But their pathway to marriage is a lot more complicated than it used to be, and a lot more painful. The seeds of future disasters are sown:

☐ The majority of people come to marriage having had multiple sexual partners. They carry infections—some incurable, some undetected—from those partners.

☐ Most have experienced sex as part of dating, not marriage, and will usually take sex more lightly as a result. They have broken off sexual relationships—or had them broken off by their partners. They are experienced at tragedy, well primed for adultery and divorce.

☐ A high percentage of people enter marriage having already conceived children. In many cases they are raising those children. In other cases they have given the children up for adoption or, most commonly, aborted the fetus. This adds a layer of complication and regret to their lives, and inevitably to their marriages.

What, then, is marriage to them? It is not the gateway to sex. It is not the gateway to children. For many, it is not even the gateway to a new lifestyle. (Living together is common—2,764,000 unmarried American couples did so in 1989.) Marriage is just the expression of a current, changeable intention.

Marriages are no longer the foundation of society they once were. One out of four children is born out of wedlock today, and an astounding 68 percent of black children are born to an unmarried mother.[9] For those lucky enough to be born into an intact marriage, the future remains insecure: one million children see their parents divorce each year.[10] Numerous studies have shown that these children are at risk for psychological problems, health problems, school problems, economic problems and just about any other kind of problem you can name. Their future is problematic. The chaos shows every sign of multiplying.

The pathway to marriage is confused and out of sequence. Now it reads,

First comes love and sex, then comes an end to the relationship. (repeat three times)

If you get pregnant, go back to the beginning.

Then comes marriage.

Make up your own ending.

2
MARRIAGE: A WEAKENED BOND

Despite sexual chaos, marriage remains. People marry as much as or more than ever. But marriages are weak in the West today, and they often break. Nearly half end in divorce.

We've grown accustomed to this tide of divorce. It has penetrated everywhere, into even the most conservative churches, into the best and strongest families. We're numb—we express our horror far more readily over AIDS or teenage pregnancies. Judith Wallerstein, who has done the best research on the long-term effects of divorce, writes, "There is an extraordinary reluctance to acknowledge [the seriousness of divorce] and its enormous impact on all our lives."[1]

No symptom of sexual chaos is more grievous or painful. Emotionally, divorce means failure at the one sexual hope we care about most. We long to bond with one lover for life. We long to establish a fruitful family: to reproduce ourselves in body and spirit. Divorce means these hopes have been crushed. They may rise again, but never in quite the way that they did in the first marriage.

It's well known that divorced fathers frequently don't pay child support, and divorced women typically have far less earnings potential. A single mother with children nearly always loses financially. The children suffer most. The poor in this country are mostly children, and a very great proportion of them are poor because their parents couldn't stay together. The economics of raising children works well only when two parents share the load. A woman's effort to do it alone is a recipe for poverty.

Even among the relatively affluent, Wallerstein has documented the enormous, lasting impact divorce has on children. She writes that at first all the "experts" were enormously critical of her findings. They were sure divorce meant merely a short "adjustment" for the child. But time and research proved them wrong: a year after the divorce things were often worse, not better.[2] After five years most children still clung to the futile hope their parents would reconcile, and were intensely angry at them for not doing so. After ten years, half the children (now becoming adults) were "worried, underachieving, self-deprecating, and sometimes angry."[3] Three out of five felt rejected by at least one of their parents. One out of four had taken a sudden, lasting drop in income with the divorce and went on "to observe a major, lasting discrepancy between economic conditions in their mothers' and fathers' homes."

Children of divorce generally come out determined that they themselves will never get a divorce. They say they'll *never* make their children suffer as they did. Yet the children of divorce are statistically more prone to divorcing. So there is a downward cycle at work.

A good marriage has always been an achievement, the most creative and difficult task most people ever attempt. The confusion and pain of today's chaotic situation makes the task far more difficult—perhaps impossible, humanly speaking, for many. When spouses have grown up abused, or without good parenting, or without good marital models, or with no instruction in how to behave toward the opposite sex, if their sexual experiences have been painful, immature failures, if they have been instructed in sex by watching TV with its endlessly mindless eroticism, if they must both work so hard that there is no time to grow together and take care of children, if adultery is always available, they will find it hard to make a marriage that anyone would want to preserve.

Something is wrong with the way we handle our sexuality if stable, loving marriages are so hard to find. Something is wrong if we keep doing this to children.

Confusion in Child Rearing

Part of the confusion over marriage is a confusion over child rearing. As a society we have enormously contradictory attitudes. On one hand we have a million and a half abortions per year. Each of those represents a child not wanted. A large, specialized abortion industry sustains our desire not to have children, even though the procedure required not to have them is, for most people, emotionally painful and morally repugnant.

On the other hand, we have another expanding industry: fertility clinics. More and more couples cannot have a baby, since we are marrying older and have far more physical problems caused by sexually transmitted diseases. Many will do almost anything to escape their childlessness.

We're not just contradictory when we think about birthing babies. We're contradictory about raising them. The bookstores are crowded with volumes of advice on how to raise children. We know more about their developmental needs than ever before. Yet affordable child care is the great cry of social progress. Interpreted, that means we want someone else to raise our children.

Affordable child care is absolutely necessary for poor, single parents. It is mere justice that they get it, if we as a society want them to work rather than to be supported by the government. Yet the ideal of child care seems to have just as much hold on those who don't "need" it.

I talked recently to a young woman, the vice president of a large corporation and the mother of several children. In conversations with younger women in the company, she had found them wondering whether they should quit their jobs to stay home with their children. The vice president was astonished and appalled. She could not imagine what would make younger women think that way. For her, the idea that a woman (or a man) would temporarily put a career on hold for the pleasure of raising children was incredible, and more than a little scandalous. That would be "wasting her potential."

How could anything have more potential than raising children?

We are a society that lauds "family values" and can't find enough money to provide inoculations for poor children. We are a society that admires Mr. Rogers yet takes elementary-age children to movies with enough violence to curl the hair on a dog.

We are confused in our attitudes toward children, and it doesn't help that so many of us raise children after marriages have disintegrated. There is simply no way children can be split satisfactorily between two parents. The trips back and forth, the symbolic struggles over money and time and discipline ("Mother says I can eat anything I want to for breakfast"), the different styles of parenting, the rivalry for the child's affection—these create chaos in the life of a child (not to mention his parents). Kids wake up to find a stranger, their mother's boyfriend, using the bathroom. They wonder whether this should be a secret from Dad, but whom do they ask?

It gets more confused when parents remarry. "Blended families" (horrible term) means children are raised in households of unimaginable complications. Is this stepparent really in charge of my life? Can he tell me what to do? Can he hit me? Since he is married to my mother, must I love him? Should I, must I, call him Dad? Is his daughter, with whom I now share a room, my sister, my rival or my friend? Frequently, these "blended families" disintegrate in a thunderstorm of shouting. They often experience violence, sexual abuse, promiscuity and, of course, more divorce.

Abuse and Rape

In a chaotic situation, people lose their sense of limits. They aren't sure what is normal, their confusion makes them anxious, and they behave erratically. Strong people may be able to deal with confusion, but weak people won't. That's why we see, in so many ways, behavior that's unacceptable by anyone's code.

Sexual abuse and incest, for example, appear to be multiplying. (It's impossible to quantify, because so much is kept secret.) We may never understand how people can do such things—they are horrifying beyond belief. But we do know that chaotic family situations allow them. Step-fathers, stepbrothers and live-in boyfriends are prime culprits in sexual abuse, and chaotic families have plenty of them. Incest is often the result of a deteriorating, violent marriage, or of unsupervised older children. Whenever people are anxious, depressed, confused and using alcohol and drugs, they are more likely to behave irrationally and offensively. Sadly, that is a description of an increasing number of households today.

When children grow up in such families, they leave home ill-equipped to deal with the chaotic sexuality of our adult world. Nothing "out there" will restrain them, train them, help them or encourage them. Instead, in a cruel and chaotic world their sexual desires will be thwarted or frustrated. They may find one-night stands easy but relationships hard.

They will find only one source of "easy" sexuality: pornography. It is no wonder that pornography has become so accessible. It may be the only sexuality some people can master. It offers ersatz sex: images made with ink or electricity, instead of real skin and real personality. Second easiest is sex with a child, unable to defend himself or herself. For people too weak to function in a chaotic sexual situation, pornography and child abuse may seem the only open possibilities.

Rape, too, is a product of chaos. The men who rape, having grown up in a household of sexual chaos, and having seen rape portrayed erotically in movies, may be confused about what sexual limits really should be. And then, they usually attack acquaintances, not strangers. Sexual chaos gives them opportunity: there is no one watching over the situation to protect young women.

Sometimes it is claimed that rape is an act of violence, that it has nothing to do with sex at all. This is only superficially true. Rape is an act of violence, nearly always against women, but anger *against* women is clearly a sexual kind of anger. It must be based in resentment, fueled by frustrating and painful relationships with women during the growing-up years, as well as sexually unsatisfying relationships with women as adults. Sexual chaos means that more young men grow up in chaotic households full of unsatisfying relationships. Sexual chaos makes it harder for both men and women to form satisfying, enduring relationships with each other. They become angry. They drink too much. They do crazy, violent deeds. They use sex as an act of anger. Sexual chaos produces rape.

That includes date rape. A man who will rape his date has, to say the least, a distorted picture of sexuality. He thinks egocentrically: he wants sex, he has a right to sex, this woman must (in her heart of hearts) want to have sex with him. He doesn't understand the slow dance of courtship: that is a nuisance, a contrivance. This is a modern world, he thinks, in which people don't have to go through such nonsense to get what they want. He feels fundamental contempt for this woman: she is only a means to his satisfaction. He is self-centered, compulsive, violent. His ego knows no bounds. It can expand indefinitely, for sexual chaos has given it no borders.

Christians amid the Chaos

Sexual chaos is everywhere we look. Its impact on courtship, gender roles, marriage and child rearing are profound, shaking our culture to its roots. Its symptoms in disease and sexual violence are most horrifying.

It would be easy to go on listing symptoms:

☐ pastors and televangelists caught in an epidemic of adultery

☐ teenagers beginning sexual activity at an earlier and earlier age (in 1986, according to Louis Harris Associates, one out of five fourteen-year-olds had experienced sexual intercourse[4])

☐ nudity and sex portrayed on network television during prime-time hours

☐ X-rated films leading the list of "most-rented" at video stores
☐ schools instructing grade-school children in the use of condoms
☐ a Supreme Court nominee's "trial" on charges of sexual harassment, featuring live, televised claims about his use of pornography

In fact, such symptoms have become a staple of conservative Christian fundraising letters. The world is going to hell in a hurry, they say; this is our last chance to defend the good old ways.

The only trouble is, the good old days weren't that good. Certainly there was a broad societal consensus that Christian morality was right, but some non-Christian beliefs were intertwined: the subjugation of women and the double standard, most notably. Nobody wants to go back to an era in which women were second-class citizens. At the very least, an adjustment and reassessment of the old ways would be necessary.

More important, we can't simply repeal sexual chaos. We couldn't even if we convinced a majority of people that it would be a good thing to do so. We couldn't because the personal tragedies of sexual chaos are being played out in our lives, in our churches, in our homes. You can plug up the broken dike after the flood, but you've still got all that muddy water to deal with. There's no simple way back to the status quo ante. We have to deal with all those broken lives—not just preach against sexual sin.

We need a two-pronged approach. First, we need to respond individually, lovingly and therapeutically to the many broken lives. We need counseling centers, battered-women's shelters, pregnancy counseling centers, marriage retreats, sex-education courses in our churches. We need support groups of all kinds. We need to provide gentle, clear guidance. We need to mediate compassion and grace.

But we can't be content just to patch up victims; we have to reduce the chaos that's producing the victims. That will take more than a knee-jerk reaction to the craziness of the modern scene. We have to understand the roots of the chaos and be careful that we apply biblical wisdom to it, not just our cultural traditionalism.

This book is primarily dedicated to understanding the roots of our current situation, and the biblical wisdom that must be applied to it.

A Call to Action

A Christian call to action is often justified with verses like these:

Marriage should be honored by all, and the marriage bed kept pure, for God will judge the adulterer and all the sexually immoral. (Hebrews 13:4)

But among you there must not be even a hint of sexual immorality, or of any kind of impurity, or of greed, because these are improper for God's holy people. (Ephesians 5:3)

God's call for sexual purity is extremely important, especially when we consider the kind of lifestyle Christians should have. I prefer, however, to begin with verses like these:

Speak up for those who cannot speak for themselves,

for the rights of all who are destitute.

Speak up and judge fairly;

defend the rights of the poor and needy. (Proverbs 31:8-9)

The LORD your God is God of gods and Lord of lords, the great God, mighty and awesome, who shows no partiality and accepts no bribes. He defends the cause of the fatherless and the widow, and loves the alien, giving him food and clothing. (Deuteronomy 10:17-18)

In biblical times powerless people were widows, orphans and aliens. Repeatedly the Bible demands justice for them and insists that God will be their defender. God cares about everybody, but he cares most about the poor and needy—since they have no one else to care for them.

Don't people claim that the Bible is patriarchal and oppressive? This contradicts them. Nobody doubts that the Bible came from a patriarchal and nationalistic culture, where men dominated women and blood was the fundamental loyalty. In his concern for widows, orphans and aliens, however, God overturns that thinking. He says the weak matter more.

Sexual chaos hurts everybody, but most of all it hurts the poor and the weak. In the midst of chaos the young, beautiful and rich will seem to thrive (at least for a time). Vulnerable people—particularly children, women and poor people—will suffer.

They do today, especially in the American ghetto, among the predominantly black underclass. All the ills that I have mentioned cluster there: AIDS and other diseases, teenage pregnancies, chaotic relationships, broken marriages, rapes, sexual abuse, violence. Marriage has all but disappeared: nearly two-thirds of black children are now born to unmarried women. Most ghetto children grow up without fathers, but with a succession of men. They fall prey to violence, malnutrition and all the confusion of poverty. Boys raised in such a chaotic situation turn violent, and they kill each other (and innocent bystanders) at such a rate that murder has become the leading cause of their deaths, and prison their most likely career.

Arlene Skolnick, in her book *Embattled Paradise: The American Family in an Age of Uncertainty,* writes, "It is possible to build a convincing case for either the optimistic or the pessimistic view of recent changes." Leaning toward optimism, she points out that "although there is much more tolerance for variation, lifelong heterosexual marriage, with children, remains the preferred cultural norm."[5]

She's right: the sexual troubles of middle America don't necessarily add up to doomsday. (Those who look closely at the spread of AIDS or the impact of divorce or the patterns of teenage sexuality can, however, paint a terribly dark picture.) But for the poor of the underclass, doomsday has already arrived. They're being shredded, and there's little prospect of improving their lives without improving their family lives.

Here's a major problem with optimism, then: so long as you say, "It's not so bad," to middle-class people, you can't offer hope to poor people. No double standard of morality between the suburbs and the ghetto is possible. Underclass people are not going to listen to middle-class people preaching a message they don't live themselves. If chaotic sexuality is a disaster in poor black society, you had better admit it is a disaster in white society.

And it *is* a disaster in white middle-class society. Archibald Hart, an accomplished Christian professor of psychology, vividly describes his own personal Armageddon in *Me, Myself and I:*

> I will always remember the day my world changed forever. Shortly after my twelfth birthday, I heard the dreaded news from my mother. I often wonder how my life would be different if it had never happened. I went to bed one day as a certain self, and woke up the next day a different self. Having chosen bedtime to tell us, Mom had asked us to go to bed earlier than usual. My young mind immediately became a little suspicious.
>
> She waited until my younger brother and I were all tucked in and then said, "Tomorrow we are leaving. I'm going to get a divorce. I can't stand it anymore."
>
> Those few words completely changed my life—not for the better, but for the worse. The impact of that decision would damage my emerging and vulnerable self beyond understanding. I would never again be the same self that went to bed that night.[6]

We owe it to God, who loves the helpless, to protect every possible child from such a disaster. To shrug our shoulders and say "change is inevitable" just isn't good enough.

3
HOW WE GOT
TO CHAOS

For fifteen hundred years, up until about 1950, Western culture had a broad consensus on sexuality. This Old Consensus, as I will call it, was often broken, and it did change with the times (when, for instance, marriages stopped being arranged by parents). But the taboos (incest, adultery, divorce) and the goal (lifelong, monogamous marriage) stayed reasonably stable.

That familiar framework is still in place, but termites have eaten at it until it won't support any weight. Nowadays when people are in trouble or in doubt, they don't rely on it. The new goal is intimacy. In their quest for intimacy, people will break the old taboos against adultery and divorce, and dump the old goal of marriage. The new taboo—what makes people truly ashamed—is sexlessness. Beyond a certain age, virginity is a horror.

But I am getting ahead of myself. Before considering what's new I want to look at why the Old Consensus fell apart after so many centuries of stability. And how did the Old Consensus come to be in the first place? It's important to understand the past if we want to decipher the present.

For or Against Sex?
Perhaps the main reason the Old Consensus broke down is that it seemed so unenthusiastic about sex. Some say Christianity, the source of the Old Consensus, is the most antisexual religion ever. They are mistaken, both because there are genuinely antisexual religions—notably the oldest forms of Buddhism—and because the Christian mainstream never went so far as to brand sex as evil. Christianity *does* have a distinct way of looking at sex, however, drawn from Old Testament Judaism.

Sex is good, that tradition says, but it is never a way to approach God or to attain salvation. The same can be said of any part of nature: the wheat crop, or a huge tree, or the sea or the sun. God made them, they should be enjoyed and appreciated, but you don't find God through them. Above all, you don't worship them.

This set the Jews apart. Many religions of the Middle East taught that one touched God through nature, and particularly through sexual ecstasy. For that very reason their temples often had resident prostitutes. Religious ceremonies could and did include sex. Such "fertility religions"—our modern term—were anathema to Jews for the very same reason that idols were anathema: they identified God with something he had made.

Hinduism is a direct descendant of these fertility religions. Until very recently it had temple prostitutes. To this day its religious dramas can be highly erotic, and its temples are decorated with symbols of penises and vaginas. This religious view of sex extends into the home. Sex manuals (notably India's Kama Sutra) have flourished since at least the third or fourth century A.D. They were never regarded as indecent or obscene; a bride might expect one as a gift for her wedding. They describe an ingenious diversity of sexual positions, along with questions of timing, caressing, kissing, biting and scratching. Sex manuals like *The Joy of Sex* are new in the West, but quite old to the rest of the world. The world's major religions—Islam, Buddhism and Confucianism—all adopted versions of these books. But the West did not.

The Greeks and the Romans were familiar with fertility religion. Their temples had prostitutes too. Their worldview held up sexual pleasure—at least for a man—as very important. Yet at about the time the Kama Sutra was composed, the Roman emperor Constantine was turning his empire toward official Christianity. It is a puzzle to many how a civilization that knew all the pleasures of divine sexuality could turn toward Christianity. Perhaps it was because the people knew from experience that the pleasures of divine sexuality are not always pleasant. The Kama Sutra and its kin were not to enter the West, for the Christian West took another course. The Old Consensus—which was then a new consensus—was being formed.

Building the Old Consensus

The Old Consensus took from Judaism the view that sex, though it comes from God, is not a way *to* God. As something made by God, sex was to be appreciated but never worshiped. This is not antisexual, but it certainly puts sex in its place. To people who considered sex divine—literally—it must have seemed strangely austere. Perhaps to new converts it looked attractively austere, the way sobriety does to a drunkard.

That view of sex made one building block of the Old Consensus. A second building block also came from Judaism, but filtered through the New Testament: a very high and strict view of monogamous marriage.

In Old Testament Judaism, as everybody knows, polygamy was common. Judaism's standards were strict—adultery was punished by death— but only to a point. You could get a divorce. Only after the exile did Jews become monogamists. Their tradition of monogamy became part of the first-century church.

The New Testament took monogamy a step further. Jesus himself spoke against divorce, which was legal under Old Testament law. New

Testament writers witnessed powerfully against adultery, against promiscuity, against prostitution, against all the "safety valves" that Greco-
Roman culture held to be harmless, even helpful, to the strength of the
institution of marriage. The New Testament's monogamy is a pure
monogamy.

And it is a loving monogamy—not merely a convenient social com-
pact, but a covenant to be filled with love as a cup is filled with wine. A
marriage might not begin with love; nowhere does the Bible say that love
should be the basis for marriage. But the Bible does insist that marriage
lead to love. The apostle Paul's repeated command is "Husbands, love
your wives."

Joining love and marriage was unusual in the first century. The
institution of marriage was familiar to the Greeks and the Romans (though
it was primarily an upper-class phenomenon). So was love. But the idea
that a man should love his wife exclusively, and have sex with no one
else, was novel.

A third building block was not an Old Testament idea, but came as
something new from New Testament Christianity: a positive view of celibacy. In Judaism, everyone married and reproduced. Not to have children
was a deep personal tragedy. The example of Jesus and Paul, however, along
with Paul's encouragement to the single life, planted a very positive idea
of celibacy in the Old Consensus. This aspect of the Old Consensus
eventually died out, but before doing so it took another shape: the idea
that sex is a dangerous influence, to be restrained as much as possible.

A Negative Stance Toward Sex
It's important to realize that the Bible was only one influence in forming
the Old Consensus. Stoic and Neo-Platonic philosophy were highly
influential in the thinking of many early Christian leaders; the whole
Greco-Roman world was saturated with ideas about the superiority of
spirit to body. Broadly speaking, they thought of their bodies as a problem
to overcome, not as a gift to enjoy.

The incarnation—God becoming flesh and blood—was a big lump to swallow for people imbued with those ideas. Most of the doctrinal quarrels of the early Christian centuries had to do with this problem in one way or another. Early Christians worked it out in their view of God—the doctrine of the Trinity—but do not seem to have worked it out fully in their view of sexuality.

The body, which is unavoidably sexual, is good. God made it, and what's more, God became it in the person of Jesus. You don't find an antibody, antisex view anywhere in the Bible. You find plenty of it, though, in the early church, and throughout the history of the Old Consensus.

The Christian mainstream never went so far as to brand sex as evil. Restricted to marriage, yes. Not as good as celibacy, yes. A danger rather than a joy, yes. But never evil. Any time sex was identified as evil—as it sometimes was by Gnostics or Manichaeans—that view was called heresy. Sex was too clearly part of God's good creation to be called bad.

From very early on, though, many Christian leaders took a negative stance toward sex. They had two reasons. One was their belief that celibacy was a higher calling than marriage. If celibacy was best, it followed that anyone who married was a second-rate Christian. (Later in this book I will discuss celibacy in more detail.)

A two-tiered view of sexuality developed. The best way was no sex. Clearly, though, most people weren't going to become celibate. For them, God's highest callings were impossible. A certain contempt for married people developed: they were seen as second-class all the way. Not only were they assumed to be incapable of celibacy, they were suspected of being incapable of fidelity. Prostitution was generally tolerated; even theologians as rigorous as Augustine and Aquinas were at a loss to imagine how a stable society could operate without "a sewer," as Aquinas referred to it. "Take away the sewer and you will fill the palace with pollution. . . . Take away prostitutes from the world and you will fill it with sodomy."[1] Most medieval cities in Christian Europe had well-organized, thoroughly accepted streets of prostitution.

The Danger of Sex

The theologians' love for celibacy is hard for us to understand today. Their second concern is easier. Christians of the Roman Empire thought of sex as a danger, and they identified the danger—Augustine in particular made this identification—as losing control. That is why Augustine thought sex was always on the edge of sinfulness: its passion was irrational.

I say that this is easier for us to understand, because I believe that we remain at the least unsettled by our spontaneous sexual responses. I think of a small boy whom his parents discovered covering his penis with his hand while he watched TV. His parents asked him why he was doing that, and he explained that "it pops up when it sees a girl." He felt that his sexuality was distinct from himself; it acted on its own. Who hasn't felt that? Who hasn't felt that he has a sexual force inside himself that is immune to reason? For Augustine, such sexual passion was the opposite of freedom; it made a human being a slave to passion.

Indeed, passion can present a frightening side. Consider a truly great, courageous and self-controlled Christian: Martin Luther King Jr. We know now that his infidelity filled him with self-loathing and depression, and that he desperately feared being exposed by the FBI. He hated himself for committing adultery, both because he knew it was wrong and because he knew it was stupid. Yet time and again he jeopardized the cause he lived and died for in the name of Christ. Why? Or fill in some other less public name—some ex-pastor who is now selling insurance. Could Satan have offered any other temptation—a million dollars tax-free, or a guest appearance on the "Tonight Show"—to make him forfeit his calling, his wife and his children?

Leaders are not the only ones so cursed by irrationality. Usually when we hear that some friend or relative has deserted spouse and children, we are stunned less by the evil of the deed than by the implausibility. "What on earth could make her do it?" we want to know.

It is a terrible sadness: we must guard ourselves in the very realm that calls us to self-abandonment and euphoria. In book 14 of *The City of God*

Augustine described this sick contradiction: "For though [the passions] are regulated by a bridling and restraining power, which those who live temperately, justly and godly exercise, sometimes with ease, and sometimes with greater difficulty, this is not the sound health of nature, but the weakness which results from sin."

Augustine's Freedom

Augustine, who was so tremendously influential in the shaping of the Old Consensus, wrote quite a lot about sex. He knew what he was talking about: he had been sexually active, as they say, before his adult conversion. It may be that guilt over that phase of his life made him negative. But Augustine is so invariably interesting that it's worth looking carefully at the reasons he actually gave for his views on sex.

Oddly enough, embedded in Augustine's pessimistic assessment of sex is the idea of freedom. For Augustine passionately believed in freedom, including sexual freedom.

Augustine's idea of a perfect world was not one in which everyone walked in lock step. On the contrary, his idea of heaven was a world in which human beings were completely, joyfully free to do whatever they wanted—and knew that what they wanted was wholly good. The tragic effect of the Fall, for Augustine, was that, left to ourselves, we can no longer do exactly what we want. "For who can count how many things he wishes which he cannot do, so long as he is disobedient to himself, that is, so long as his mind and his flesh do not obey his will? For in spite of himself his mind is both frequently disturbed, and his flesh suffers, and grows old, and dies; and in spite of ourselves we suffer whatever else we suffer, and which we would not suffer if our nature absolutely and in all its parts obeyed our will" (*The City of God* 14). The fact that we must guard ourselves, and even do battle with ourselves, the fact that our bodies take their own course, even getting old and dying though we don't want them to, marks our loss of radical freedom. Nowhere is this more evident to Augustine than in our sexual conduct, where all through life our organs embarrass us by disregarding our will.

Augustine thought that sex should be rational. A man or woman who wanted to be celibate should have no difficulty with that. A man or woman who was married should feel attracted only to his or her spouse. Freedom, for Augustine, is the ability to decide in a thoughtful way what kind of life you want to live, and to live it.

But sex doesn't work that way. A celibate man doesn't stop feeling sexually attracted. A married woman doesn't feel attracted only to her husband. Often sexual passion leads them in a totally irrational direction. So it happened with Martin Luther King, and many others.

Augustine's solution was to try to rule passion out of sex—or at least limit it. Sex should be for procreation, he said, and nothing else. But of course, the church fathers knew as well as we do that passionless sex is all but a contradiction in terms. So they had a skittish view of sex: necessary, at least potentially good, but invariably troublesome and dangerous. Theoretically, at least, they weren't against sex. But they certainly gave that impression.

The theologians' insistence that sex behave rationally—that is, that it lead to its supposedly proper end of children, rather than passion—led to strange twists. Aquinas, for instance, considered masturbation worse than rape, since rape might still lead to the proper end of procreation, while masturbation was pure passion.

They also developed a very negative view of women. They themselves were men, so their dangerous passions were bound up with women. It was easy to slip into blaming women for providing an opportunity for temptation.

People who emphasized the dangers of sex were all too apt to slip into thinking of the body itself as evil. Odilon of Cluny, writing in the eleventh century about sexual intercourse, asked, "We, who would be loath to touch vomit or dung even with our fingertip—how can we desire to clasp in our arms the bag of excrement itself?" One cannot be further from the attitudes of Eden, where Adam and Eve were "one flesh," naked and unashamed. Odilon is closer to the attitude taught in the Buddhist scriptures, where a monk was to contemplate the human body as a butcher would look at a cow's carcass; he should think of it as "encased in skin and full of various impurities: nails, skin, teeth . . . stomach, excrement, bile, phlegm, pus, blood, sweat, tears."[2]

To confront the dangers of sexual passion, medieval Christianity developed detailed manuals that priests used in taking confession. Some manuals instructed priests to delve into the minutest detail of a person's sexual life, including the frequency, positions and sensations of intercourse. The priest, representing God, was to supervise the most intimate relations of married life. (A modern therapist might ask similar questions and wield similar authority for a similar reason—to make sex serve the good. But there is this important difference: therapy is voluntary, while confession was not.)

The Reformation and Beyond

The Reformation changed Protestant Europe's view of sexuality. Marriage, which had been second-rate and unspiritual, became the norm almost overnight. Celibacy almost disappeared. For Martin Luther, celibacy was virtually impossible, and certainly not a way that led anyone closer to heaven. Perhaps more than Luther's theorizing, his example—a turbulent yet happy marriage after a lifetime of celibacy—had a very great impact. The Reformation also put an end to priestly confession, and in a practical sense freed people's sexual lives from the church. Since the Bible said nothing about positions, frequencies and sensations, Protestant ministers did not either. What married people did in their bed was a matter to be settled with God, not the pastor.

Yet the Reformation did not really change the fundamental building blocks of the Old Consensus. Particularly, Protestants retained the suspicion of passion. Luther's ambivalence shows clearly in his concluding sentence to *The Estate of Marriage:* "Intercourse is never without sin; but God excuses it by his grace because the estate of marriage is his work, and he preserves in and through the sin all that good which he has implanted and blessed in marriage." Sex remained a danger—a danger which marriage contained and to some degree transformed.

The Puritans, despite their reputation, were relatively positive about sexuality, for they had a warm understanding of the value of family life. Yet even for them, and much more as interest in sexuality increased during the Victorian age, the subject of sexuality remained hemmed in by caution. It is so still for many Christians. They have an immediate seizure of conservatism when sex is mentioned. They are rule-oriented. "Life, the puritan argues, may not be quite as much fun if you accept his perspective, but it's a lot safer," writes Andrew Greeley.[3] So the Old Consensus taught us.

The Sexual Revolution

Between 1945 and 1965 this Old Consensus, after centuries of stability, broke up. The sexual revolution had been taking shape for decades, especially among the avant-garde. However, most people still trusted the Old Consensus: first comes love, then comes marriage, then comes Mary with a baby carriage. Adultery and divorce were wrong; society was clearly against them.

Then, suddenly, sexual freedom broke out of the province of free-thinking intellectuals and artists, and very quickly became the common person's view. This was triggered not by an intellectual breakthrough but by two medical discoveries: penicillin and the Pill. The first could cure syphilis, which is a highly contagious, deadly sexually transmitted disease. Sleeping around no longer meant risking your life. The second prevented babies far more efficiently than previous methods of birth control, and thus suggested that sex's connection to family was unnecessary. Sex could be, for the first time in history, separated from life-and-death consequences. Understandably, people's views of sex became more liberal, and so did their behavior. They seemed to have nothing to lose.

But there was more than medical technology behind the change. The Pill and penicillin liberated people toward a faith they already had begun believing in: sex as savior.

Faith in God had been dying ever since the Enlightenment. People only vaguely believed in the coming of the kingdom of God. The authority of the Bible was suspect. They turned toward human reason for guidance and recognized sex as one of the great joys of human life. Beginning in the early nineteenth century, thinking people became fascinated by sex. The first utopian "free love" colonies were formed, and even though only a few people joined them, a great many people discussed them. True, there was greater caution than ever. Victorian doctors cataloged the varieties of sexual perversion and warned of the dangers of masturbation as never before. (It wasn't particularly conservative Christians who did so; progressive thinkers led the way.) Yet even in this caution you can recognize the fever of enthusiasm. Sex was terribly, terribly important, more significant than people had thought it to be. They turned more and more to sex for answers about the meaning of life. As they did so, caution seemed less and less adequate. The question changed from "How can we control sex?" to "How can we most enjoy sex?" Sex, modern people came to believe, is all about pleasure and intimacy—not caution. In fact, caution interferes with pleasure and intimacy.

Revolution appropriately summarizes what happened. The Old Consensus didn't get an overhaul. It got overthrown. All three building blocks were thrown out completely. A cautious view of sex was traded for an enthusiastic view of sex. The positive, pure view of the institution of marriage was tossed. Marriage became incidental; love and pleasure were key. Lost, too, was the understanding that sex is not a pathway to God. Our culture began almost to worship sex. The questions people had once addressed to God—"What should I do with my life? Where can I find meaning?"—they increasingly addressed to sex, and the experts on sex.

The Playboy Experiment: Rejected

The sexual revolution spurred a variety of views on sex, and the Playboy experiment was only one. Sex was good, Playboyists insisted, and the only bad thing was not enough of it. The Playboy philosophy urged people to act on their blessedly natural sexual urges, without restraint. Hugh Hefner probably did the most to convey this philosophy to the masses, but others said essentially the same thing with more sophistication. They often referred to Sigmund Freud and his theories about sexual repression, but their real intellectual ancestor was Jean-Jacques Rousseau, who thought that humanity in the wild state was naturally good and happy, but was spoiled by society. That such dreams should endure for two centuries is remarkable, for to this date no happy humanity unspoiled by society has been found. (An occasional "wild child" is found in the forest, but it has proven difficult to call inarticulate, animalistic behavior happy and good.) Men and women inevitably live in society, and societies always have ways of organizing their sexual behavior. Yet Rousseau's myth has astonishing staying power. One can still hear speculations about, for instance, how many people would be homosexually oriented if society had no influence on them; or whether humankind is naturally monogamous. Humankind is not naturally anything, if by "natural" you mean without social imperatives.

A good number of people tried life by the Playboy philosophy, and some are still trying it. But we can now consider the experiment rejected. Long before any full-scale disaster broke out, people began losing interest in the Playboy philosophy. They discovered that they wanted love more than sex. "How to have a good relationship," not "how to have good sex," became the editorial foundation of most general-interest publications.

What made the Playboy experiment a failure for most people was not AIDS or any other sexually transmitted disease, but loneliness. Sex researchers Masters and Johnson chipped in by pointing out that sexual pleasure was highest in a caring relationship. A new ethic began to evolve: the Ethic of Intimacy. Let's examine this new ethic with care.

4
THE ETHIC
OF INTIMACY

S ome time ago I was having lunch with two older pastors. When I told them I was writing about modern sexual ethics, they shook their heads, smiled and said they didn't realize there were any. To them, any ethic but the Old Consensus is a nonethic.

Traditionalists may have a hard time seeing how the Ethic of Intimacy is different from the Playboy experiment: both seem to lead to rampant hedonism. But it's important to see that the Ethic of Intimacy is a well-meaning attempt to guide sexuality in the right direction. For one thing, it is moderately positive about marriage. You don't see so much written now about the crippling inhibitions a puritanical society imposes; the Old Consensus is no longer an enemy so much as an unrecoverable past.

Sexual freedom is a given in the new ethic, but it is not an end. It is to be guided by the ideal of intimacy.

Intimacy is the guiding light of most Westerners' sexual lives. Intimacy is not love, exactly. It is a state that two people may feel for a night, or a month, or a lifetime. Though women's magazines contain a good deal of advice on it, intimacy is a quality you cannot precisely describe. Most people would say, I think, that you know it when you feel it. The Ethic of Intimacy offers no behavioral absolutes, but many attitudinal absolutes, such as openness and caring. It is these attitudes and the personal feelings between two people that make up intimacy.

The Old Consensus offered behavioral absolutes, for its linchpin was marriage. You could define right and wrong as precisely as you could define the institution. Today the demarcations are blurry, either coming in or going out of relationship. Couples are expected to first sleep together, then live together in a kind of trial marriage, then finally (if things work out) ratify their state in a ceremony. Everything depends on how intimate they feel. That is why some women's magazines do not use the terms *husband* and *wife* much any more. The current terms are generic: *partner* or *lover*. This is not antimarriage. It is mildly positive about marriage. But marriage does not come first. Intimacy does. And only the individual is capable of judging what "intimate" is.

Actually, the Ethic of Intimacy has been developing for centuries, in the rising significance of romantic love. As a smitten girl in Rodgers and Hammerstein's *Carousel* put it: "What's the use of wondering if he's good or if he's bad? . . . He's your feller and you love him. That's all there is to that." A great many people who supported the Old Consensus accepted that, even wept over that. But in doing so they were undermining the Old Consensus, which insisted that love was important, but not more important than inquiring into a lover's character.

The Ethic of Intimacy takes Rodgers and Hammerstein just one small step further. If a person's character means nothing in the face of love, then surely the niceties of a marriage ceremony mean even less. What matters is simply the particular feelings inspired when two people are together.

Everything depends on that magical spark of intimacy—its presence or its absence.

Seven Features of the Ethic of Intimacy

In order to understand the way people apply the Ethic of Intimacy, we need a more detailed understanding. They do more than surrender to their feelings. They do so within a particular set of assumptions, so fundamental that they are rarely articulated.

1. *An invariably positive view of sex.* Any threads of the old belief that sex is dangerous seem thoroughly gone. Sex is wholly good if carried out in intimacy, and mostly harmless in other contexts. One-night stands still happen, and they are pardoned as excusable, almost inevitable. However, one-night stands are far from the ideal. A person searches for that fragile state of intimacy wherein sexual intercourse is an expression of caring. There and then, sex is a gift from heaven. It seems to be the only part of human life that is utterly incapable of harm.

2. *The independent individual.* Always, even within intimate relationships, two watchful individuals retain their independence. They consider their own needs paramount. Picking up at random a copy of *Glamour,* I find Bette-Jane Raphael writing, "I believe that we all have the right to decide what to disclose to our partners. . . . No one, not even my partner, is entitled to know everything about me. Why should he know that I once stole crayons from Woolworth's when I was a little girl?"

In the same issue, in a monthly column entitled "Sexual Ethics," Priscilla Grant writes, "True lovers give each other permission to retreat; no lengthy explanations or excuses are necessary."

Intimacy, by the new ethic, never controls the individual. No covenant binds one person to another through absolute obligations. An individual's primary covenant is always to him or herself.

3. *Compatibility.* If you ask what creates intimacy, the answer in a word is "compatibility." This does not particularly mean sexual compatibility. Time was when the rationale for couples' sleeping together before marriage was "how else will they know whether they are sexually compati-

ble?" By now, though, nearly everyone knows that couples are not sexually incompatible in the way a Ford transmission is incompatible with a Honda drive train. They are compatible or incompatible in personality and values.

Nonetheless, this is usually seen as relatively fixed. Compatibility just happens—you "click." Of course that introduces a problem: people change, so couples who are compatible today may not click tomorrow. That is why you cannot be rigidly against divorce or adultery. Few favor divorce or adultery, but against incompatibility, who can stand? Happy, lifelong monogamy is less a triumph of the will than a miracle of compatibility. You hope that you and your lover can stay balanced on the bubble indefinitely. But you admit that the forces of fate may ruin your plans. According to the Ethic of Intimacy it is naive and arrogant to pledge your love "as long as we both shall live." Better to say "as long as we both shall love." If it happens, it happens.

4. *Sex is a private matter.* What you do and whom you do it with is a matter for you to settle for yourself. Fundamentalist Christians can live how they please, but they have no right to tell others how to behave. People's sexual behavior is their own business, unless the person happens to be running for president. Thus a church that expels a member for committing adultery can be sued, and many people believe it should be, for they see sexual conduct (apart from sexual harassment or abuse) as none of the church's business.

The privatization of sex received a huge boost when penicillin and the Pill came out of the laboratories. Both fostered what can now clearly be labeled an illusion: that sex, thanks to medical breakthroughs, has no impact on society. In an era of millions of abortions, of multiple generations of unwed mothers on public support, of epidemic sexually transmitted diseases, the idea that sex is a strictly private matter is incredible. Yet it continues to exert a powerful force.

5. *Sex has no necessary personal consequences.* The Old Consensus treated the move from virginity to sexual experience as a change in a person's very being. A virgin was a different kind of person from a

nonvirgin. Today people think the impact of sex is almost infinitely variable. Intercourse is thought to mean different things to different people at different times. Whether someone is a virgin or not, whether someone has had one partner or dozens, tells you very little about him or her.

The broad assumption is that most people will have sex with numbers of people while trying to "click." Even when the relationship is a failure, at least they are learning about life. They are getting to know their own sexual responses. Some experiences will be good and others not so good. But every time, with every new partner, you have a chance to start afresh.

6. *No double standard.* Today women are treated exactly the same as men. If you wink at one's infidelity, you should wink at the other's.

7. *Sex requires maturity.* The Ethic of Intimacy is situational; each person must consider a number of variables in figuring out what to do, and what is right for one person in a particular situation might not be right for another.

Applying situational ethics requires maturity and wisdom, especially when sex and its emotions are involved. Many people doubt whether kids are capable of it. They feel uneasy about this doubt, because of feature 4: *sex is a private matter.* What right do they have to impose their opinions on anybody, even their own children? Ellen Goodman, writing in *Ms.* magazine about the ambivalence of parents trying to convey a new morality to their kids, quoted a woman with a thirteen-year-old daughter: "We're trying to communicate a situational norm, like, it's okay under certain circumstances. If you both honest-to-God want to. If you think you'll be in each other's lives for a while. If you are responsible. If you use birth control, if you are old enough, if you won't get hurt, if you have a wholesome sexual experience." Commented Goodman, "Her list of 'ifs' extends into the air."

Despite this uncertainty, an uneasy consensus has emerged that kids sixteen and under are too young for sex and should be told so. (This consensus is, however, consistently undermined by the contention, championed by Planned Parenthood, that widespread sexual activity is inevitable among teenagers, and that however much adults might like teenagers under seventeen to stop engaging in sex, they will continue. Therefore the only sensible course of action is to dispense contraceptives and abortions freely.)

The Victims

What can we say about the Ethic of Intimacy? Should we shout frantic warnings about the dangers of AIDS? That seems unlikely to work—and likely to backfire if a cure is found.

Then what can we say? Christians can hardly be against intimacy. We value it too. What we must say, I think, is that the Ethic of Intimacy is too weak—too weak to deal with the powerful human urges, often destructive, that make up our sexuality. It is like walking a lion on a leash. Sometimes it goes where you want it to. Sometimes it will not. Sometimes it turns around and devours you.

The Ethic of Intimacy is inherently vague; under sway of emotions you can convince yourself that anything is intimate. And there is a strange current of passivity and fatalism in it—a surrendering of self to the gods of eros—which undermines human dignity. For if compatibility is the key to intimacy, we are at the mercy of circumstance. Either we are with the right one or we have missed and must start over.

It is a strange paradox that modern people who insist on their sexual freedom can think of no way to use their freedom other than to change partners. The Christian ideal places a person's will at the center: love is work to be done, and intimacy is to be created through persistent self-sacrifice. The Ethic of Intimacy puts our efforts in a much less important place.

Because of these weaknesses, the Ethic of Intimacy does not live up to its own standards. It does not create or enhance intimacy. It merely glorifies it.

If someone asked what is wrong with the Ethic of Intimacy, I would say simply, "There are too many victims." I would say, "Three hundred thousand babies born each year to unmarried teenagers, many of whom will spend their lives in poverty. One and a half million abortions. Twelve million cases of sexually transmitted diseases (many incurable, some deadly). Millions upon millions of divorces; millions upon millions of children growing up with one parent. About three times as many divorced women now as in the seventies. (Divorced men remarry women on the average ten years younger than the women they divorced. The older women have a much smaller chance to remarry.) And on the whole, less intimacy and more loneliness than ever before."

All these statistics are regularly in the newspapers. As a society we are reeling: burdened with an underclass of ruined families, staggered by millions of abortions and terrified by sexual epidemics. The wide-eyed promises of the sexual revolution, that all would be well once Victorianism was uprooted, can hardly be made with a straight face any more. Yet nobody (except fundamentalist evangelists on TV) seems to put cause and effect together.

We manage to shrug off the victims because they are mostly people who "don't matter"—the poor, the young, the uneducated, the slightly-too-old. And the damage is diffuse. Not everybody suffers. Plenty of people sleep together before marriage, even live together before marriage, and yet form strong, durable relationships. Practicing homosexuals make outstanding, sober-minded citizens. Men and women leave their families to form new marriages and seem to gain peace of mind.

Some do, that is. Many don't. Only an extraordinary, willed amnesia enables us to forget millions of victims.

Our society regards victims as unavoidable. Experts stress the medical cures, the legal and economic reforms that will minimize the pain. Certainly minimizing pain is right. But the huge number of casualties is not inevitable. There have been few times in all history, in fact, when so many sexual casualties have been present in any society.

How the Ethic of Intimacy Affects Teenagers

A critical test of any ethical system, particularly regarding sexuality, is how it affects the young. They are highly vulnerable, for with them

nothing is settled. And they are our future. How does the Ethic of Intimacy
filter down to them? How does it affect them?

Personally, I have encountered much of the pathos of our situation as
I've read thousands of letters from kids. For years I have written an advice
column for teenagers in the pages of *Campus Life,* a Christian magazine.
In addition to reading their letters, I have kept up on sociological statistics
about teenage sexuality. In this chapter I rely primarily on statistics found
in the comprehensive study *Sex and the American Teenager,* by Robert
Coles and Geoffrey Stokes. Other studies show similar results. The Ethic
of Intimacy does percolate down to teenagers, and it leads to experiences
I think are very unlikely to foster lifelong intimacy.

1. *An invariably positive view of sex* reinforces what needs no encouragement—kids' interest in sex. Kids get the message that sex is wonderful
and right whenever two people are intimate. They assume this includes
them, since at age thirteen more than half say they have been in love, and
by age seventeen or eighteen over 80 percent believe they have already
experienced love.

Few teenagers are truly promiscuous, sleeping with just anyone.
Two-thirds experience sex for the first time with their boyfriend or
girlfriend. Once they begin they nearly always continue. Only 6 percent
of the nonvirgins surveyed had gone for more than a year since last having
intercourse. While some do experience "secondary virginity," it's not the
common pattern.[1]

Why do they continue having sex? Because they like it. Many of the
girls experience disappointment or pain initially, but ultimately about
two-thirds of both boys and girls who have had sex report enjoying
intercourse either "a great deal" or "a large amount."[2] Thus the Ethic of
Intimacy is experienced: intimate sex is good—at least it feels good.

This sense of intimacy is naive and short-lived, however. About half
of the fifteen-year-old girls surveyed by Robert Coles and Geoffrey
Stokes said they expected to marry their most recent sexual partner.
Unfortunately, almost none of them would. (Boys seem more realistic:
82 percent said they did *not* plan to marry their partner. Evidently their

sense of intimacy did not necessarily include telling their partner this fact.)[3]

2. *The independent individual* means that these kids experience a series of short relationships. Indeed, independent individuals of all ages are less likely to stick together, since they have no overarching loyalty to hold them together. This tendency is, however, far more pronounced in teenagers, because they are rapidly changing, because they move when their parents do and because many eventually go away to college. Only 14 percent of teenagers' sexual relationships last more than a year—about as many as last a week.[4] Since half the sexually active teenagers start sexual relationships in their early teens, they run up quite a string of sexual partners by the time they are old enough to leave home. One should not conclude that these relationships are casual, or the breakups relatively painless. One staple letter I receive is from the teenager trying to get over a relationship, agonizing and fantasizing over it as much as two or three years later. Often they get involved in other sexual relationships in an attempt to make up for the loss. We have no instruments to measure pain, but my impression is that these kids feel as devastated as do adults in divorce court.

3. *Compatibility* brings an almost frantic concern with finding "the right one." Letter after letter comes to me asking for formulas: how do I find the right one, how do I know if I have found him, how can I tell if this is true love or merely infatuation? Kids have long had fantasies about meeting Mr. or Ms. Right, but they used to daydream at a relatively harmless level. Today they go to bed together. They lack a future orientation toward which to dream and pine and mentally prepare. They think more existentially. If you happen upon the right person, you can be intimate. It's more a matter of being at the right place at the right time than a matter of choosing one sterling person to love for life.

4. *Sex is a private matter* means that kids have a tremendous amount of respect for others' decisions. Take this letter:

A friend recently confided in me that her boyfriend and she have been sexually active for almost a year. Because we are close friends, I want to be supportive of her but I'm not sure how right it is for me to not discourage her from making love with someone whom she says she loves. I know I have no right to control her morals. It was hard to answer when she asked me whether or not I thought it was "wrong"— because what I may consider wrong for myself may not apply to her.

A sizable minority of kids hope to stay virgins until they marry, but they usually consider this a purely idiosyncratic decision. On one hand these kids benefit from sexual privacy: their peers might razz them a little, but usually not much. (Here I am talking about public pressures. Between a boy and a girl, alone, a good deal of pressure can be applied.) On the other hand, privacy means that kids feel very strongly that sex is *their* decision, and none of their parents' or their teachers' or their pastors' or even their friends' business. Society's collective caution disappears. Sexual and romantic urges gain in significance.

5. *Sex has no necessary consequences* means that kids are often confounded by their own experiences when they find consequences, emotional or physical, staring at them.

They have, after all, seen hundreds and hundreds of couples go to bed on TV and in the movies. None of them got pregnant. None of them got AIDS or other STDs. None of them found themselves trapped in a guilty pattern they can't escape. Yet these are the real-life consequences of teenage sex. Not many sixteen-year-olds have thought beforehand about what it would be like to have herpes for life. A tone of astonishment and shame pervades their words when they write to me after discovering that they are pregnant or have contracted an incurable disease. Their own physical suffering is only one part of their regret. They cannot imagine how they will someday tell a person they want to marry.

Even more common are psychological consequences, among which is the fact that once they have begun participating in sex many find they cannot stop.

I have a big problem. About four years ago I met a really nice guy who had just moved to my neighborhood. He was the first guy I really loved, and the first guy who really loved me back. We started going together about six months after he moved here. We had a very serious relation-ship—we were sexually active.

We broke up one year ago, and we're still sexually active. We still care about each other a lot, but not enough to be doing this. Besides, it's wrong.

He goes away to college this fall. I don't know if that's good or bad, because I couldn't imagine never seeing him again. I still care about him a lot. He's my best friend. I'm very jealous of him and other girls he sees or dates. I feel I have a right to be.

I want to be happy, but it's been so long since I have been! We've tried to stop having sex, but so far it hasn't worked. I've prayed, but nothing seem to help. I don't have anyone to talk to. I have learned a lesson, though: sex can be a very bad habit, if you start when you aren't with the person you will be spending the rest of your life with.

When teenagers surrender their virginity, their lives are changed. If they once imagined themselves sleeping only with the love of their life, they now usually must adjust to the reality that they will have a number of sexual partners. By the time they get married, they will have a sexual history to tell.

6. *The end of the double standard* means that teenagers today make no distinction between the morality of girls and that of boys—even though their parents often still do. No doubt this is a good development. None-theless, those who become sexually active still encounter the double standard of biology. Only about a third of sexually active teenagers use any effective form of birth control, which means that a great number of American girls (perhaps a third) get pregnant while they are teenagers. Though the boy often sticks with the girl through the immediate trauma, teenage relationships almost never endure beyond the crisis. Girls con-tinue to be victims, with or without the double standard.

7. *Sex requires maturity* suggests that kids are not ready to experience sex—at least not in their early teens. But the weakness of a situation ethic shows up: those least capable of mastering a situation ethic are often most likely to believe themselves capable. Nobody yet has managed to con-

vince a majority of teenagers that an experience that is right for twenty-five-year-olds is wrong for fifteen-year-olds. That sounds too arbitrary. Besides, it is probably in the nature of teenagerdom to believe oneself fully grown up.

Consequently, the adult consensus that sixteen or younger is too young for sex has made no observable impact. At fifteen, a quarter of the teenage population, both boys and girls, have already had intercourse.

The New Double Standard

The impact of the Ethic of Intimacy on teenagers is disastrous. Not only does it expose them to disease and pregnancy, it is a terrible foundation for stable marriages and positive male-female attitudes.

Not everyone sees the situation so balefully as I do, of course. Kathryn Burkhart is typical of "experts" in the way she states the optimistic case.

Making explorations into their sexual feelings and into sexual interactions with another person at the age of 16 or 18 does not mean that today's teenagers will be any better or worse off than we were when we did the same things at the ages of 20 or 25. Some of them will make right choices for themselves, and some will make wrong choices. They will have relationships that affect them in a variety of ways. But when they behave sexually, when they respond to another person, they are doing something that human beings have done for as far back as the history of humans extends itself. Even though each sexual experience is individual and intimate and unique, in it, we become part of the human race, linked to humankind, past and future, regardless of what language we speak, what customs, beliefs, cultures, attitudes or perspectives we bring to the experience.

Today's teenagers may be aware earlier, they may be exposed to more, they may make decisions sooner than they would otherwise, but they'll most likely find their way through the hazards and the squalls and the ways of the world as well as we did. And in their own way.

Burkhart also gives her prescription for teenage ethics: "It seems to me that adolescents of all ages should be encouraged to have foreplay and to defer intercourse until they are extremely comfortable in their own bodies and very much at ease about themselves and their sexual partners. Teenagers should think about their own requirements for sexual intimacy and have great respect for their own feelings and values."[5]

Her words are an excellent reflection of the vagueness of the Ethic of Intimacy. The great reassurance, phrased in the rosy tones of organic unity, is that people have been having sex for a long time, and these kids are doing it too. The values kids should follow are "to be extremely comfortable in their own bodies . . . at ease about themselves . . . aware of their own requirements" and "to respect their own feelings and values." In two words, "Be careful." What this will tell a kid after half an hour in the back bedroom I will leave you to guess.

This is no proof that we are seeing the first sign of the Decline and Fall of the West. Teenagers still believe in marriage; a lot of them (perhaps half the girls) hope to be virgins at the wedding. The family is a durable institution, and history indicates that it has survived worse enemies than vague ethical standards.

But no one can doubt that there will be many more casualties, particularly among the most vulnerable members of society. Already it is clear that kids from divorced families are almost twice as likely to engage in sex as teenagers whose parents have remained together.[6] It is not difficult to imagine that these same kids will form weak marriages, and that in turn their kids will have a long series of sexual partners culminating in more weak marriages. I am not suggesting that people who engage in premarital sex are necessarily any worse, morally, than their peers who do not. I am asserting that those who build their sexual lives around the vagueness of intimacy will be less likely to build strong marriages. To build strong marriages—a difficult thing under the best of circumstances—you must put marriage at the top of your sexual values.

For Lack of a Counterculture

I don't see any immediate prospect of turning our culture away from the Ethic of Intimacy. Its assumptions go too deeply into people's unconscious attitudes, and they are reinforced daily by the media. I believe our strategy ought to be the formation of a sexual counterculture. We ought to say our piece, loud and clear, to the world. But we ought to place an even stronger emphasis on making certain that Christians—particularly young people—gain a sense of group identity while taking a separate course. They ought to know that "we're different"—and consider it a blessing to be different.

The strongest predictor of whether teenagers will have sexual intercourse is whether they are influenced "a large amount" or "a great deal" by religion. About 18 percent of teenagers say they are, and only 10 percent of these have had intercourse.[7] This is not a matter of nominal religion. Kids who go to church, even kids who claim to be "born again," don't behave much differently from other kids. It is a question of how teenagers themselves have responded to God. In this committed minority we find, perhaps, the beginnings of a counterculture.

I fear, though, that many Christians have almost fallen for the Ethic of Intimacy. In responding to the Playboy experiment we have put great emphasis on the joys of love and unconsciously downplayed the demands of the institution of marriage. We have become sympathetic to divorce— not merely compassionate toward those who divorce but sympathetic to the reasons they do it. We have acknowledged that marriage can be very difficult, but not said much about what benefit justifies this difficulty. We have collaborated with the emphasis on compatibility by building a theology of "the right one," whom we say God will reveal through a sense of inner peace. We have communicated to our children our fear of premarital sex (though we still, strangely, sprawl in front of the TV, where by one count six extramarital sex encounters are portrayed for every one of sex between spouses). But we have not communicated, I think, the great value of marriage, an institution that demands so much of us in such clear, hard lines.

The Ethic of Intimacy is destructive for adults as well as teenagers, and in the same ways. It simply is not strong enough to train our wild, contradictory, variable sexual and romantic impulses; it works, rather, to help us justify doing what we wish. For some—particularly the attractive, the well-off and those in their twenties and thirties—this freedom will be pleasant. But within society as a whole, and particularly among the less attractive, the poor, the young and the slightly-too-old, the Ethic of Intimacy creates too many victims. And even those who seem to thrive do less well than they ought: they should be learning how to deepen love in the face of difficulties, rather than merely enjoying the freedom to "click."

The appeal of marriage lies in its toughness, in its rigorous, invariable demand that each individual choose one person, and one only, to marry, and in its demand that each one sacrifice to create within that marriage a garden of intimacy. Make no mistake: a pure, loving monogamy forces us to do things we would rather not. But we need its strength and clarity to drive the powerful force of our sexuality toward lasting intimacy.

The challenge posed for us by the Ethic of Intimacy, I believe, is not only to preach to teenagers against premarital sex, but to preach to all ages the immense value of a pure and loving monogamy—and to live it so well as to make it attractive.

5

SEXUAL
SALVATION

The drums exploded and the songs of the singers rose to heaven
as two priests from the interior of the temple led forth
a priestess. . . . She was an exquisite human
being, a perfection of the goddess Astarte. . . . Urbaal
stared with unbelieving eyes as the naked girl
submitted herself to the crowd's inspection. . . .

"She is Libamah," the priest in charge announced, "servant of
Astarte, and soon in the month of harvest she will go to
the man who has this year produced the best,
whether it be barley or olives or cattle or any growth
of the soil."

"Let it be me," Urbaal whispered hoarsely. Clenching
his fists he prayed to all his Astartes.
"Let it be me. . . ."

"Through them life will be born again!" the chorus chanted.
JAMES A. MICHENER, *THE SOURCE*

The Ethic of Intimacy fails the test of experience: it promises
intimacy, but delivers chaos and hurt.

Looking at it pragmatically, though, is not enough. You cannot
understand the sexual revolution without seeing its profoundly religious
nature. Just like the priests in Michener's tale of ancient fertility religion,

the sexual revolution promises that life will be born again through sex.

The sexual revolution is explicitly secular, and many of its experts would be scandalized to think of themselves as promoting a religious view. But one does not need much imagination to see that the sexual revolution attempts to recast reality so that sexual experiences can give meaning to ordinary life. That sort of enterprise is just what religion is about.

William Stafford writes,

Hugh Hefner's career is a graphic example of how far this creation of reality may need to go. Inventing a "philosophy" to rearrange his own values and relationships was straightforward enough. Then came the magazine, the houses, the clubs, as a sort of monastic order for "free sex," where an entire culture of voyeurism and sexual play could flourish, where other perspectives could not interrupt the constant stimulation. The order was quite evangelistic; few Americans' values are now unmarked by the Playboy Philosophy.[1]

Playboyism is, as we have seen, a brief moment in the history of the sexual revolution; it stands, anyway, under strong suspicion (like more than a few religious movements) of using high-minded double-talk as a cover for less noble objectives, such as increasing the opportunities for men to "score." But the same religiosity can be found in other leaders of the sexual revolution: gravity, self-certainty, greatly disinterested and scientific motives, outrage and disgust against the oppressive powers from which we can be freed, the constant, spiraling assumption that a mystery and a secret in our sexuality can be (must be) found out, for our liberation.

The Pill and penicillin triggered the sexual revolution, but in and of themselves they do not explain it. After all, the Pill and penicillin are available worldwide, but not all societies have followed our lead toward sexual liberalism. Technological advances made the sexual revolution feasible, but some deeper impulse had to drive it.

Even the Pill and penicillin did not develop in a vacuum, as though an Einstein musing in his laboratory suddenly conceived them out of nothing. They were developed through years of cooperative research at great expense, because of deeply felt societal desires. Penicillin could be discovered and developed only by a society deeply committed to curing disease—that is, to controlling certain effects of nature. The Pill could be developed only by a society fascinated by sexuality as a subject for medical investigation—and thus committed to controlling sexuality (as a part of nature). Our society, more than any before, is committed to a relentless scientific probing of nature, not simply in order to understand it but in order to control and transform it.

This holds true in genetics (we cannot be content to understand our genetic makeup, we must master gene-splicing) and atomic physics (not merely understanding of the universe, but nuclear power and bombs), and no less does it hold true of sexuality. Masters and Johnson not only studied the functioning of the clitoris, they pioneered "sex therapy."

The Pill and penicillin gave confidence that we can master disease and reproduction. Freud, or pop-Freud, gave confidence that we can control sexual guilt. Suddenly humankind seemed really able to choose without limit: to do whatever it wanted with whomever it wanted, without having to fit into a rigid framework instituted by nature or God. Oh yes, God. It was necessary to have confidence about him, too: either that he had evolved into a benign dignitary or that he had ceased to exist altogether.

Why This New Thing?
The theme of autonomous mastery ("You will be like God") is not a new one, of course. Since Adam and Eve human beings have been experimenting with ways to make God superfluous. Nonetheless, the sexual revolution is something new under the sun. Historians and anthropologists increasingly recognize its uniqueness. Lawrence Stone, the Princeton historian, writes, "Before now, sexual libertinism has been confined to narrow elite circles, often around a court. Its dissemination among a population at large, as has occurred in the last 20 years, is a phenomenon unique in the history of developed societies."[2]

Historians do not use the word *unique* lightly. Some undeveloped societies—notably in Polynesia—apparently institutionalized promiscuous premarital sex, it is true. But a consistent mark of developed societies is that they value premarital virginity and strongly protect the bond of marriage. Our society, alone in history, is attempting to change this.

This revolutionary newness requires some accounting, and it is interesting to notice how various writers have explained it. Some claim that our uniqueness comes because we are the first generation to have effective birth control. Before, extramarital sex meant children born out of marriage; now sex is freed from that constraint. "After centuries of guilt and repression, the bait of sexual pleasure has at long last been separated from the hook of reproduction. We finally have acquired sexual freedom," claims Irene Kassorla in *Nice Girls Do.*[3]

But it is increasingly obvious that the Pill has not eliminated the "hook" of unwanted pregnancies; we have more unwanted children (as well as more abortions) than ever in our history. Nor, when you think about it, is it apparent why pregnancy has to be a "hook." Not all societies have thought of pregnancy and sexual pleasure as implacable rivals. Some might say that the possibility of children is one of the chief pleasures of sex.

Another common explanation: the sexual revolution is really not new at all, but merely the return to a normal way of thinking about sex. According to this hypothesis, what was "new" was the vicious censorship and moral hysteria of earlier times. Victorian prudishness, it is commonly said, brought massive repression, and our twentieth-century sexual revolution is merely a reaction against it.

This hypothesis, however, does not match the historical evidence. The French historian Michel Foucault, in his multivolume history of sexuality, makes a convincing case that Victorian sexual moralizing and our twentieth-century sexual revolution are actually different facets of a consistent, growing attention to sex (or, more exactly, to talking and confessing about sex) that began more than two centuries ago. We have not, Foucault claims, returned to a pre-Victorian approach to sex; we have carried on the Victorian obsession with sex, only in a different way.

Historian Peter Gardella makes a further point about the nineteenth-century American doctors and religious figures who pronounced on sexuality, stigmatizing masturbation and suggesting that married couples should ideally have intercourse once a year. These men and women are usually presented as mossgrown conservatives. In fact, Gardella says, they were from the most liberal, optimistic strand of society. They expected medicine (which included programs of sexual control and diet) would do through a scientific health program what the church in centuries of preaching had been unable to do: make people good. Essentially, their intentions were not very different from those of modern-day sex experts; only their technique was different. A vast, deep cultural movement has long been under way: a movement to study, understand and control our sexuality, in order to save ourselves.

Sex Transcending Nature

People sometimes describe the sexual revolution as an attempt to get back to "natural" sex. But even a casual glance at the current literature of sexuality will show that it is at certain points extremely opposed to anything natural. For instance, if you listen to Dr. Ruth, you will hear her unfailingly ask her callers whether they use birth control. It amounts to an obsession with her. She writes, "I would like this country to put its resources toward finding a perfect contraceptive. . . . Good contraception is important for the peace of mind people need in order to abandon themselves into the never-never land of sexual excitement and pleasure and ecstasy without having to worry that somebody may get pregnant. It is foolish to allow the danger of an unwanted pregnancy to enter into the lovemaking experience."[4]

Fear of unwanted pregnancy clearly can indeed interfere with the pleasures of recreational sex. But even more clearly, we are not then talking about "natural" sex. Pregnancy goes naturally with sex, if anything does. The sexual revolution is not a revolution against an unnatural view of sex; it is a revolution in favor of a studied, calculatedly unnatural sexuality. The need for endless volumes on technique, for unnumbered clinics run by scientific "sex therapists," for monthly educational articles in *Reader's Digest,* to say nothing of our fascination with recorded images of beautiful individuals pretending to have intercourse—scenes included in most popular movies—makes it very obvious that our age is not at all interested in letting sex take its blessedly natural course, but in stimulating it, studying it, teaching it, therapizing it and controlling it until it meets some ideal. It is no longer credible to claim that we are temporarily concerned with overturning the rigid proscriptions of Victorianism, and that once we have purged ourselves of moralistic poison our fascination with sex will decline to some healthy, normal level. Year after year the concern, anxiety and fascination of sex grow deeper.

Foucault writes that we have come "to direct the question of what we are, to sex."[5] Gardella puts it more broadly (and perhaps more as an American): "Our sexual ethic has a religious quality that it could only have inherited from the Christian zeal to overcome sin and to experience salvation. As Tom Wolfe observed, Americans seek in orgasm 'a spark of the Divine.' "[6]

So how do we explain the sexual revolution? It is, quite simply, a religious revolution. As Christian belief has faded, another faith has been needed to take its place. Science has served in this quest for meaning, but has not provided the fundamental direction. Science has taken its cues, as a good servant of society, from a deeper, religious drive. Western society, which once viewed sex as a source of danger, at its best confined within marriage and used for the production of children, now views sex as a source of limitless pleasure and personal discovery, at its best freed from the inhibiting possibility of children or any other social consideration. If in the past sex was unrealistically viewed as demonic, it is now viewed as messianic. We study sex as a savior: it will tell us our true nature and save us from meaninglessness.

Sex and Religion
Sex as savior has an astonishing quality to it. C. S. Lewis caught it when

he wrote, "You can get a large audience together for a strip-tease act—that is, to watch a girl undress on a stage. Now suppose you came to a country where you could fill a theatre by simply bringing a covered plate on to the stage and then slowly lifting the cover so as to let every one see, just before the lights went out, that it contained a mutton chop or a piece of bacon."[7] Lewis said such behavior would show that something had gone wrong with people's appetite for food.

But there is a subtler implication. It would be strange for people to crowd into a room to see a piece of bacon uncovered, but perhaps no stranger than what one sees in any Christian church when people take Communion, lovingly holding and distributing tiny bits of bread and drops of wine. In religion, simple things become infused with a greater meaning. They gain a fascination and an emotional importance far beyond their practical function. So it is with sex in our time: it has become a sacrament.

If it seems strange to speak of sex in such language, that is a heritage of Western society. Because Christianity condemned fertility religions, we have been shielded from their influence. Most of the world's great religions placed sex—often extramarital sex—in a central, sacramental position.

Hinduism, of all the great living religions, is most directly a descendant of the fertility worship Michener dramatized. The oldest forms of Buddhism, by contrast, have a strongly ascetic cast; monks are celibate. But over centuries Buddhism came to take different forms, and Tantric Buddhism made even more of sex than Hinduism did. Group orgies were a form of union with the gods.

Taoism and Confucianism, more philosophic than theistic, viewed the male-female balance (yin-yang) as fundamental, and thus proper sexual relations as religiously crucial. A man observed a very careful sexual regimen with his wives and concubines, being careful to absorb as much yin (female) essence as possible while conserving his own yang (male) essence. The result of this quasi-scientific sexual regimen was supposed to be perfect harmony.

In all these, and in other less-known religions, it was very natural for people to think of sexual energy as related to a divine, life-giving energy.

The Model of the Prophets

We need to understand the religious nature of the sexual revolution because it gives important clues to how we ought to respond. Many Christians react with horror to the sexual revolution. They refer to "filth" and moral degradation, as though it were obvious that displaying sex openly amounted to filth. Such a response does not answer: the faithful of the sexual revolution consider open sexuality something to be proud of, not ashamed of.

We could learn a better response from the Old Testament prophets. They were quite familiar with sex religions, but they did not condemn them for their sensuality. It was not their lewdness that offended; rather, it was the fact that they were directed toward something other than the one true God. When Israelites indulged in fertility religion the prophets didn't charge that they were hedonists, but that they had deserted their true husband, Yahweh, for another lover.

How had they deserted God? They remained a very spiritual people. They still worshiped at Yahweh's temple. What was so wrong with accepting some of the good points in other people's religions? Didn't all the world know that sex was part of fertility, and fertility was what made the crops grow, and the crops were what made life possible? Was it so wrong to honor this in a religious context?

The prophets' answer was that there is only one God to be worshiped. He has no rivals. He alone saves; he alone provides blessing and wisdom.

Sex-centered religions, ancient and modern, look elsewhere for blessing. They look to powerful forces—the power of pleasure, of fertility, of maleness and femaleness. These forces gain a divine status. One seeks to release their power in one's life.

The faithful Israelite's first question about sex was not how to gain power or happiness from it, but how sexuality should reflect faith in God. On this basis, before all others, Christians must evaluate the sexual revolution. To the extent that it is an assertion of human potential apart from God, it is wrong. When it worships the created as though it were itself divine, it is wrong. When it tries to gain meaning and transcendence through a human activity, it is doomed to failure.

6
THE NEW
SALVATION

What we need is a new morality freeing sex from
the old anxieties, the old inhibitions, and from the social and
sexual supremacy of one sex over the other,
all of which are damaging to the full enjoyment of sex
for both females and males. A new sexual ethic will have to be
as definite as was the old one; but it ought to be
a morality flowing from man's inner values, not one imposed
on him by authority or tradition. . . .

In short, it will have to be a sexual morality which results in
a secure bond, free of any bondage. It will have to be a morality
that facilitates sexual, emotional and social
relationships in which each partner finds deep satisfaction
of his dependent needs; but within which he can
also afford to develop his individuality to the fullest,
due to the pleasure each partner finds in watching the other
achieve his self-realization.

BRUNO BETTELHEIM,
"ABOUT THE SEXUAL REVOLUTION"

I quote from Bettelheim, though I could easily offer more striking examples of sexual utopianism. Bettelheim is far from an excitable radical. He is the very essence of a calm, cultured, controlled psychoanalyst. Yet there is a strong scent of utopia in these paragraphs, as in much that is written about sexuality these days.

They promise salvation here and now—a heaven on earth. They expect this salvation to be invented by our generation, acting on its own inner values rather than any traditional understanding. It would not be quite accurate to say that sex is to be our salvation. Rather, we are to be our own saviors, drawing up our code of conduct and belief, and centering our quest for salvation in the region of sexuality—in sexual pleasure, in intimate relationships providing "a secure bond, without any bondage," in maleness and femaleness that will want and do only the best for each other.

The modern, secular version of sexual salvation has a loosely defined set of substitutions for traditional religious categories:

- ☐ for heaven we substitute pleasure (or intimacy)
- ☐ for finding God we substitute finding oneself
- ☐ for forgiveness of sins we substitute forgetting
- ☐ for the Ten Commandments we substitute therapeutic values
- ☐ for good deeds we substitute "good people"
- ☐ for Scripture we substitute science

For heaven we substitute pleasure (or intimacy). Pleasure is what we think we were made for, what we long to experience, and what we work and suffer for. (As with heaven, too, we never quite arrive, we are always on our way.)

Irene Kassorla's *Nice Girls Do,* which spent twenty-two weeks on the *New York Times* bestseller list, offers hard-sell evangelism for this gospel: "How many of you have experienced the optimum in sexuality: *complete* emotional and physical satiation? And how many among you have ever heard of an orgasm called the 'maxi'? Few women in the world have."

She continues by promising bliss:

You're the only one who can make it happen *for you.*

You deserve the pleasure.

You deserve to be a *happy, fulfilled* woman. . . .

Every nerve ending can become sensitized to the sensual experience: your shoulders, your cheeks, your fingers, your toes—everything! You'll be able to orgasm as easily with someone touching your back as you will when someone touches your clitoris. And afterwards you will revel in complete contentment and peace with yourself—feeling energetic and refueled, ready to tackle a busy schedule at work or at home. . . .

Every woman reading this book can learn how to make her sexual hopes and fantasies become living realities. You can stop comparing yourself negatively with other women; you don't need to feel different or inadequate anymore. You can be the exciting, sensual woman you've envied in books and seen in films.[1]

Having described heaven, Kassorla gives her definition of tragedy. "The tragedy of most sex is that it ends with the first orgasm."[2]

Others would claim that the greatest pleasure is possible only in marriage. Sex therapist Paul Pearsall, director of education for the Kinsey Institute, asserts that "super marital sex is the most erotic, intense, fulfilling experience any human being can have. Anonymous sex with multiple partners pales by comparison. . . . No form of extramarital sex can compete with super marital sex, and once this lesson is learned, spouses having affairs may begin cheating on their 'lovers,' and having 'intramarital' sex with their husband or wife."[3] Josh McDowell, whose Christian seminars on "Maximum Sex" have attracted large college audiences, presumably agrees.

Intimacy amounts to another kind of pleasure—the pleasure found in a person (as distinct from a body). It is broader and deeper than the pleasure Kassorla describes—it offers emotional and intellectual as well as sensuous intensity—but it is still pleasure found through sexual relations. As such, it can be defined only by the person experiencing it. He or she alone knows what feels good.

The pathway to sexual pleasure, however, is not straight. Therapist Alexander Lowen notes, "There is available to the public an extensive literature that describes the sexual techniques of different cultures, East and West. Unfortunately, it offers no insight or help for the problems of sexual unhappiness that are presented daily to physicians, psychiatrists, and marriage counselors."[4] Sex therapists deal increasingly with people who, despite great sexual sophistication, find little pleasure in sex.

Those who don't thoroughly enjoy sex believe that something crucial is missing from their lives. A Christian who had lost his enjoyment of worship might feel a similar emptiness—though only if he were an unusually committed believer. In sex, we have no shortage of committed believers. They believe that they were made for intense sexual pleasure. Lacking such pleasure, they are sure they are headed for hell.

For finding God we substitute finding yourself. In traditional Christianity, heaven is where God is. The joy of his presence defines the joy of heaven. Modern sexual salvation offers no God, or considers him a peripheral figure. So what do people find in the heaven of pleasure? They find themselves.

That is, they find feeling creatures, "in touch with their feelings," aware of their own drives and able to express them freely. (Old definitions of humanity as thinking creatures, or as moral creatures, seem out of date.) Of course, sexual pleasure is the apex of feeling. Therefore it offers the key opportunity for finding oneself.

In *Intimacy: the Essence of Male and Female* Shirley Luthman puts it this way: "Maximum growth for the individual is dependent on his capacity to express who he is—*which means his feelings*—clearly, congruently, and spontaneously"[5] (italics added).

A happy relationship, then, is two individuals glowing with the healthy confidence born of finding themselves. The emphasis is not on their delight in each other, but on their satisfaction with how a shared life affects each one's individual happiness.

Your partner can never make a strong claim on you. Only your feelings have a claim on you. Essentially, you are feeling pleasure in finding yourself, and finding yourself in feeling pleasure. Others mainly provide the context.

What happens when a partner betrays you? The fear of betrayal is a constant undertheme in pleasure-seeking lives. No one can guarantee that her partner will find her a fulfilling experience tomorrow. So intimacy is undercut by a wariness toward other people—a sense that ultimately they ought not to be depended on.

For the forgiveness of sins we substitute forgetting. Dr. Ruth, the well-known sex therapist, makes clear that some deeds, like unfaithfulness in a "closed" relationship, ought to be avoided. Nonetheless, one phrase rings through her advice: "It happened." She advises a man who has cheated on his wife and consequently caught herpes: "These things do happen. For you I think the most important thing right now is not to think about regretting for the rest of your life, and not to think what you ought to have done, because it happened. I think what you ought to do is take your wife out for dinner, or a ride, and then go home [and talk]. Don't do it someplace outside, because if she does want to be angry, or cry, or whatever, she should have that freedom either in the car or at home."[6]

Herpes made truth-telling inevitable in this particular case; the husband's lesions were so obvious he could not even undress in front of his wife. When unpleasant truth-telling can be avoided, however, Dr. Ruth thinks you should. "It happened" means "Let's try to overlook it if we can. If not, let's talk about it. Either way, let's go on from here without dwelling on the past any more than is strictly necessary."

Sexual mistrust and betrayal make deep wounds. The sexual revolution offers no way to deal with these wounds, except by "working them through" therapeutically. It's true that secular therapy urges you to remember, to dredge up wounds from childhood and get in touch with your feelings about them. The goal of remembering, however, is not repentance or forgiveness. The goal of therapeutic remembering is forgetting—to come to the point where you've grieved over what happened enough to drop it.

For the Ten Commandments we substitute therapeutic values. The values that guide a therapist include to accept people as they are, to be sympathetic as you help them understand and accept themselves, to assist them in making their own choices. These are quite distinct from more traditional values, which clergy once were known for: to teach people to want to be right, inwardly and outwardly; to help them measure themselves against God's standards (the Ten Commandments); to foster the choice to love and obey God, and to discourage any other choice. The moralist is a surgeon, cutting away cancerous tissue and setting broken bones. The therapist is a midwife, optimistically assuming that amid the chaos of any life something is being born, something that only needs assistance.

The therapist's tolerance, acceptance and patience can be a great relief to wounded people. The demands and judgments of a family, a spouse, a church, an organization or a business are relentless; the therapist provides a fifty-minute refuge from society's judgments in order to explore the reasons behind and the possibilities of escape from whatever is going wrong.

When the therapist's office grows to consume the whole world, though, we enter a very different situation. Then, it seems, nothing can be right or wrong except tolerance or intolerance. James B. Nelson, perhaps the best-known liberal theologian of sex, writes, "God's radical, unconditional, and unearned acceptance of us is a fitting contemporary translation of justification by grace."[7] If so, that acceptance is not the same as the therapist's. The therapist chooses not to judge behavior which he would surely have to judge if it occurred in his home; he suspends judgment. If his client tells him that she kills and eats neighborhood dogs, the therapist covers his shock and mildly says, "How do you feel about that?" He does the same if his client tells him that she slept with fifteen men last week. God's acceptance is quite different: based not on willed amnesia, but on mercy. His judgment is not suspended, but absorbed at great personal cost in the death of his dear Son. The sin is confronted in all its deadly power, so that while the accepted sinner escapes that power, he or she knows even while being accepted that what he or she has done is tragic and deadly.

Nelson further writes, "If it be argued that we can reject the sin without rejecting the sinner, the question must be asked, but what if the so-called 'sin' is as much a part of the person as the color of the skin?"[8] To this question we must rejoin: what other kind of sin is there? Sins are not clothes that we put on or take off. Sin sinks its roots into the heart, and we sinners are powerless to dig it out. Righteous acceptance of sinners is grounded only in Jesus' agonizing death for sin. This is quite at odds with contemporary attitudes, according to which sins (if they exist at all) call not for repentance, but for a therapeutic hug and a word of pseudograce: "That's okay."

For good deeds we substitute "good people." Our secular society, while admiring good deeds (those of Mother Teresa, for example), finds it increasingly hard to specify any behavior as required. Good deeds are negotiable; what is nonnegotiable is that you be a "good person."

A bestselling book made this quality explicit in its title: *When Bad Things Happen to Good People.* The title apparently made instant sense to millions of people. In modern minds a category of "good people" exists. Such people do not deserve to have bad things happen to them. Every bad thing they receive is an injustice.

But who are these good people? Are they saints? Perhaps they are in Rabbi Kushner's thinking, but I daresay most of his readers thought of good people as "people like me." They don't do anything bad enough to make the 6:00 news. They have good intentions, even when they mess up.

"Good people" are those whose spirits are good. But there's no necessary connection between good people and good deeds, between good people and intact families, between good people and good relationships. Bad things "just happen." "Good people" aren't responsible, they are victims. Our society turns out to be, not materialistic as sometimes charged, but spiritualistic. In sexual matters particularly, we are unable to think seriously about the consequences of acts done by the body. Otherwise we'd have to ask: What's so good about these "good people"? How come they do such bad things?

One could cite many examples. The consequences of divorce on children, of promiscuity on the growth of poverty, of sex-saturated television on teenage pregnancies—all are briefly looked at, then passed over. The most penetrating recent example has been the inability of modern moralists to grasp the implications of AIDS. It is considered terribly bad form to emphasize that the disease could never sustain an epidemic without behavior traditionally considered immoral. That would seem, in that classic phrase of no-fault modernity, to "blame the victim." Can anyone doubt that these victims are "good people"?

For Scripture we substitute science. Sexuality can be analyzed and explained through laboratory experiments like those Masters and Johnson undertook, or through questionnaires like Kinsey's. If Scripture is considered at all, its truthfulness will be examined by asking whether it agrees with scientific findings.

The scientific approach would be impossible, however, if sex were concealed in modest silences. Science requires full disclosure. Kinsey needed people who would answer personal questions. Masters and Johnson needed people who would copulate in the laboratory. A climate of complete sexual candor is essential if we are to understand sex through science.

This climate is sometimes abused, most people admit—by pornographers, for instance. There is no changing it, though. Ironically, during the same period that sex became viewed as a strictly private matter, it also began to dominate public life. Sex is a private matter, but you can hardly turn on the TV without hearing about it. We live in a constant bath of depersonalized, imaginary, highly provocative sexuality. To modern people, this seems normal; they are barely aware of it.

Different Religions, Different Lives
Joanne is an attractive woman who heads data control for a large food distributor. She took several years to accept her divorce, for she had really loved Nate. They reunited several times before giving it up for good.

Now she is quite cynical about the conservative sexual ethics she grew up on. "It's hard to believe I swallowed that whole line," she says to a friend. "When I think of the energy I put into saving my virginity, it stupefies me."

For two years now, Joanne and Hank have been together. Once, when he developed a stomach ulcer, she moved in with him, but feeling not quite right, she went back to her own apartment when he recovered. A tall man with a striking shock of gray hair, Hank teaches ethics in a business school and is sometimes quoted in *Newsweek*. Everybody likes him, and Joanne feels fortunate to have him. Or almost to have him.

One weekend Hank didn't answer the phone; he admitted later, after only a little resistance, that he had been with his former wife. He didn't offer any apologies, and Joanne felt she couldn't make a scene—she didn't own him. It turned out not to be too rare an event. Once he took a working associate to ski in Switzerland for a week.

"I guess it bothers me," Joanne confesses, "because my biological clock is ticking. Oh, maybe I am a little jealous, but I can live with it. However, I would like to have kids, and I think Hank would make a wonderful father. I just don't feel settled. I certainly don't feel solid enough to go ahead and have a child. Do you think that's just an excuse? I mean, do you think my upbringing is getting to me?"

In Joanne you can see how great a difference our theology of sexual salvation makes. The Old Consensus told her one thing, which still hangs in the back of her mind. The new sexual salvation, which she has absorbed from magazines, TV and bestselling books, tells her something quite different.

It tells her to look to her sexuality—her sexual pleasure, her intimacy with Hank—for meaning in life. Through these pleasures she can find herself, learning not to deny her feelings.

It tells her she has no claim on Hank. She can only express her feelings. If those feelings go with Hank's feelings, they will continue together. If not, they will move on.

It tells her that compatibility is the foundation of her relationship to Hank. Apparently they fit. Or do they? Possibly her restlessness derives from some feelings that she is not in touch with. Joanne needs to explore these feelings, to know whether she and Hank really are compatible. (If they're not, it's best to end things quickly. You can't change yourself to please a man, and it would be wrong to try to change him.)

It tells her to remain resolutely disinterested in what went wrong in her marriage. "It happened."

It tells her to brusquely reject anyone who suggests that her living arrangement with Hank is wrong. She will not be dominated by anyone else's morality. How she lives is her business, no one else's, and only she can know what is right for her.

In the end, it creates a different life for her. She was raised to a life controlled by commitments, both to God (she would obey his directions) and to a partner (she would strive to create a good marriage with him, no matter what the challenges). Now she has a life controlled by her feelings, and the feelings of a partner, as they change from day to day.

The Modern Challenge

This modern challenge has already changed the way in which Christians talk about sexuality. Church seminars today can be quite explicit and idealistic about sex, in a way that seemed impossible a short time ago. Yet this new idealism often seems to mimic secular optimism. It seems to accept the secular challenge on its own terms.

SEXOLOGIST: Why are you Christians so uptight about people get-
                     ting a little pleasure?

SEMINAR LEADER: We're not. Frankly, we're all for pleasure. Our God
                     is a God of pleasure. The Bible says he made all things
                     for us to enjoy. The fact is, a Christian marriage has the
                     potential for sexual pleasure like you never heard of.

Which may be true. The trouble is, in accepting the hedonist's challenge we seem also to accept the hedonist's premise, that pleasure is the ultimate aim of sex. I am not certain that Christians will win a contest of hedonism, and I am certain they should not want to enter one. It is not possible to accept the premises of a secular salvation and then staple on God.

The Old Testament prophets, I have suggested, are a model of how to respond to a religion of sexual salvation. Their persistent condemnation of fertility religions was not over their sensuality, though sanctified prostitution must have been horrifying to conservative Israelites. Nor was the prophets' critique pragmatic—that the crops didn't really grow any better when you fornicated in the hill shrines. Their critique was centered on the contention that there is only one God. Isaiah made that point in scornfully describing how idols were made from a log of wood and then tacked down to the floor so they wouldn't fall over. Such a "god" is no God. There is only one God, only one who created the world, only one who gave us our sexuality. He alone deserves worship. He alone can rightly demand total allegiance. He alone can save.

To understand the biblical view of sexuality, you must ask what sex has to do with God—the God who revealed himself to Abraham, to Moses, to David and finally in and through Jesus Christ. We have spent enough time trying to analyze and understand the modern view of sexuality. It is time to look afresh at God's view, as presented in Scripture.

7
A HAPPY MARRIAGE

We are in a sexual crisis. Chaos rules in the lives of countless individuals. Pain is felt everywhere, penetrating every community, every family, every church. More than ever, we need to hear from God.

To some people, the phrase "God's Word" suggests killjoy restrictions and rules. But the Bible does not begin to speak about sex with "Thou shalt not." It begins with a description of joyful, sensual abandon. It begins with a love story.

The first chapter of Genesis reverberates with the regular drumbeat of "good" as God creates the universe. At each stage he looks creation over and pronounces his pleasure. But then he announces something unsatisfactory. "It is *not good* that man should be alone." God's company was not enough for Adam; the first man needed the companionship of another creature. In solving this problem, God presented all the animals to Adam as potential partners. None was found suitable.

So God made a partner for Adam—Eve—and presented her to him. Adam's reaction was immediate and passionate: "This is now bone of my bones and flesh of my flesh." He felt kinship, and it drew him to her.

Sometimes people say that marriage works because of the differences between the sexes—the way in which male and female, as opposites, complement each other. Genesis's story brings a very different emphasis. Of course the two are different: they were even made differently. Yet it was because of their similarity, not because of their differences, that they were drawn to become intimate partners in the Garden.

Their intimacy is summarized in lovely and unforgettable terms: "The man and his wife were both naked, and they felt no shame."

Genesis 1:27 relates this community of male and female to God himself: "And God created man in his own image, in the image of God he created him; male and female he created them." Something of God is seen in Adam and Eve. As Adam could delight in Eve because she was like him, so God finds particular delight in this man and woman because together they are like him. There is fellowship between the three.

Don't let anyone tell you that the Bible is antisex. Eden introduces a very idealistic picture of sexuality. It is a brief sketch of a story, yet one we all recognize, because we have lived it—at least in our dreams. From the time that they first become sexually aware, boys and girls daydream about meeting each other in a kind of Eden, naked and unashamed. The real world of sex and marriage can be dreary and heartless, but the hope of replicating Eden begins anew with each generation.

The Origins of Marriage
Having reported Adam's passionate reaction to Eve—"this is bone of my bones"—Genesis goes on to say, "For this reason a man will leave his father and his mother and be united to his wife, and they will become one flesh." This verse was later quoted by both Jesus and Paul. It is not a

comment on Adam and Eve, who had no parents, but on marriage as a persistent human institution. It answers the question "Why on earth do people get married?" Marriage is a remarkable fact of all civilizations—most remarkable of all when seen against a tribal background, in which ties of children to their parents are tremendously strong.

What is stronger than the link between children and their parents? The link between a man and a woman, who forsake their parents for someone outside their family ties, with whom they become "one flesh." And why do they undertake this tremendous social revolution? The cause can be found in Adam's spontaneous reaction: This is my kind of creature. With her, I can be at home. Humans were made for unashamed nakedness—*intimacy* seems a weak word to describe it. Longing for it, we marry.

And usually we have children. Genesis does not mention procreation in its verse explaining the fundamental motive for marriage (2:23). Rather, childbearing is mentioned in Genesis's first chapter, as a command in the context of a blessing: "God blessed them and said to them, 'Be fruitful and increase in number; fill the earth and subdue it' " (1:28).

We do not marry to have children, but to find "bone of my bones." God calls married people, however, to the responsibility (and blessing) of children. Does this mean it would be wrong for a couple to decide never to have children? It means at least that a couple ought to have a very good reason for such a choice. Marriage and children are meant to go together.

We should remember, however, that the command to be fruitful was given when birth control did not exist. The command had nothing to do with whether a couple should use the Pill. Rather, for Adam and Eve the command must have meant "Enjoy sex with each other, and be careful to care for, protect and train the children God gives you as a result." God affirmed that children were part of his blessing, and part of the task given to a man and a woman.

I have heard elderly people, both men and women, say that having and raising children was the most significant thing they did with their lives. Children give us a sense of making progress in the world, of "subduing" the earth, as God commanded Adam and Eve to do. Husband and wife share this sense of significance, and it draws them closer together. The "one flesh" of sexual intercourse gains a wider and deeper meaning as the two partners work out a shared life—including the shared work of children.

So, in Eden's story, Adam ultimately recognized his wife as more than "bone of my bones." While remaining a joy to him, she would become more—a source of life to others. It was this realization that impelled him to give her the beautiful name Eve, meaning "living" (Genesis 3:20).

Eden's story resonates in our experience this way, too. Marriage begins with a small, closed circle: a woman, a man and the God who gives them to each other. Their eyes are only on each other. "This is bone of my bones." Yet God has a greater blessing in store for them. He lifts their eyes beyond each other. As partners he invites them to "subdue the earth"—that is, to create a humane society. As bearers of God's image, they are to impress his image on all that surrounds them. Marriage begins with the impulsive longing for another, but comes to the creative task of shaping the world. We do it through children, through work, through church, through neighborhood, through public service. We do it together.

That is why marriage answers sexual chaos. It puts God's stamp on society, making peace where there is no peace, producing order and love and joy where before "the earth was formless and empty." Go look in any community, however wrecked by chaos and pain. Whatever order and joy you find are likely to stem from the loving bond between a man and a woman, extending outward through the family they create.

The "thou shalt nots" of Old Testament sexuality relate back to this primary good. Marriages need protecting, particularly from the danger of adultery. They are the primary way—not the only way, but the primary way—in which our sexuality reflects God's goodness.

How Marriage Reflects God's Glory
As it was in Eden, so it is today: good and loving marriages reflect God's glory. Like a well-cultivated field, they shine with his goodness, love and faithfulness.

First of all, marriages built on the biblical pattern tend to be loving. The partners know they are called to live caringly, even when their spouse doesn't deserve it. They're not to think of themselves first, and what they're getting out of the relationship. I'm not saying that married people live up to this standard—I know I don't—but at least those who understand Christian marriage acknowledge that they ought to. They try. After all, Jesus gave his life for us when we least deserved it. His example, if it is followed, creates a climate of love and acceptance that can heal many wounds. In fact, it does. Sociologists who gather statistics can find the results. Where you find committed marriages, you find whole people.

We have a handwork motto on our bedroom wall that says it well: "To love and be loved is the greatest joy on earth." Quite evidently, real love must swallow faults, pain, difficulty. That may be hard, but it is also ultimately happy. Who does not want to live in that kind of gracious climate?

Second, Christian marriages tend to be secure. Divorce has certainly invaded every sector of our society, including the church, but those who understand Christian marriage are likely to resist it. They are more likely to marry intending a strong commitment "so long as we both shall live." Such people don't have to reevaluate their marriage's future every time they have a fight. They can put their energy, instead, into long-term solutions to their problems. To put it crassly, knowing they will have to put up with each other for the rest of their lives, they feel compelled to improve the marriage. Security breeds happiness, both because it reduces anxiety and because it frees both partners to invest wholeheartedly in their relationship.

Third, Christian marriages will tend to feel safe from disease. Just a short time ago, that seemed a negligible consideration. Today, in the era of AIDS, it seems very significant. Anxiety about diseases can affect a person's view, indeed a society's view, of sex. Bruno Bettelheim, writing before AIDS or herpes came into view, commented, "The Victorian attitude that sex is ugly cannot be fully understood without reference to venereal disease. It is such an ugly and scary sickness that loathing of it extended back to the act through which it was transmitted. . . . Modern youth cannot really understand how their grandparents could have viewed sex as ugly, because they have never experienced the haunting fear of venereal infection."[1] Now some modern youth have begun relearning that fear. But it is not necessary to do so. The plagues of AIDS, herpes and other sexually transmitted diseases are something people committed to Christian marriage will read about in the newspaper more than something they experience or worry about for themselves. They alone can have a truly positive and wholesome view of sex.

If any marriage is loving, secure and safe, it will usually add a fourth quality: good sex. The couple may not match the widely advertised feats of sexual gourmets, any more than meals from the average kitchen match those displayed on TV cooking shows. But people who are committed to live caringly, who believe their marriage will last and who aren't worried about disease are likely to experience satisfying sexual relations. Well-known sex therapist Helen Singer Kaplan writes, "Sexual dysfunction is unlikely to occur in comfortable, caring relationships because there is little performance anxiety when [partners] trust and care about each other."[2]

Of course, sexual problems can occur in very loving and secure marriages, while very bad marriages can be highly erotic. But that's not common. In general, pleasurable sex is grounded in security and love.

There is no precise way to measure happiness—you can only ask people how they rate themselves—but people committed to loving and lifelong marriage will tend to be happier. From a purely pragmatic point of view, marriage has a lot to offer the world. More important, strong marriages show the character of God. He created our sexuality, making women and men to bond with each other in unashamed nakedness. When we follow that plan, our lives will tend to display God's goodness and love. A good family, which begins with a good marriage, is a signpost of heaven.

Desire and Domination
I say our lives will "tend" to display God's goodness. Unfortunately,

Adam and Eve's story did not end in the Garden. They sinned, and their estrangement from God marred their partnership. The curse God pronounced to Eve suggests a result with which we are all too familiar. "Your desire will be for your husband, and he will rule over you" (Genesis 3:16). As Derek Kidner has put it, "to love and to cherish" became "to desire and to dominate." So it has been ever since: intimacy trying to coexist with sex drives and assertions of power.

What exactly changed at our first parents' fall into sin? Did the physical nature of their sex life actually change? Augustine imagined that it must have, since he could not imagine God pronouncing good on the kind of sex he had experienced. He imagined Edenic sex as having no passion. "With calmness of mind and with no corrupting of the integrity of the body, the husband would lie upon the bosom of his wife. . . . No wild heat of passion would arouse those parts of the body, but a spontaneous power, according to the need, would be present. . . . Thus not the eager desire of lust, but the normal exercise of the will, should join the male and female for breeding and conception."[3] This does not sound, to modern people, like much fun. In fact, it does not sound much like sex. It sounds like a theologian's strained attempt to honor the name of sex without admitting its true character.

Augustine's idea of passionless sex is an easy target. Could he not see that Adam's first reaction to Eve was a far cry from this? Nothing in Scripture suggests that passion was a product of sin.

There are other explanations of what changed with the Fall. Mary Stewart Van Leeuwen suggests that sin manifests itself in gender roles: the male desire to dominate, the female willingness to accommodate and evade responsibility.[4] Others have speculated that the male tendency to fantasize about depersonalized bodies—shown in the distinctively male penchant for pornographic photos—may have originated at the Fall.

What clearly did change was human beings' definition of themselves. We began to think of ourselves as self-driven gods, treating other human beings, our own bodies and even God himself as instruments for our own pleasure. Where once Adam and Eve shared fellowship with each other and with God, now we think of ourselves as over and against others. It is as though they had been made by us and for us alone; their role is to make us happy. That is why, from our point of view, they exist. When they fail to live up to our expectations, we are angry or hurt.

Like Adam, people hide from God because they fear he will interfere with their lives; like Adam, they blame their spouse for their own failings. Fallen people think they are the center of the universe. The result is too often the "not good" of Eden—for each person is alone again.

The examples are everywhere, if we want to look for them. The man chasing a beautiful woman to gain ego satisfaction and body pleasure in the catch. The group of women making points for themselves by disparaging their husbands. The boy who has conceived a child but considers it the girl's problem, not his. The wife and husband not speaking to each other, furious for each other's failure to provide happiness.

All of us, in all our interactions, slide toward regarding others as merely instruments for our pleasure. The story of Eden, of mutual unashamed nakedness, of passionate joy in discovering another, of the shared task of children and "subduing the earth," is thoroughly confused by this contrary story of people who think, each one, that they are gods, knowing good and evil without anyone's—least of all God's—direction.

The story of Eden offers a beautiful picture of marriage as it is meant to be. It is not, however, God's last word on marriage. Another story shows how marriages—real, hard marriages made by sinful persons—can reflect God's glory.

8
A HARD MARRIAGE

I f I understand what the Bible says about sex," my friend Ruth says, "I'd sum it up by saying that sex is meant to be connected. It's not supposed to be isolated from the rest of life; it's an expression of the connection between two people. And marriage is the ultimate connection. But if that's so, why are so few Christians sexually happy? Why doesn't the theory match the reality I see?

"Every marriage that I'm close to is, under the surface, unhappy. In every one, both the husband and wife would say in their most honest moments that they would be happier married to someone else."

Ruth doesn't insist that the marriages she knows are altogether typical. She lives in a sophisticated college town. Maybe marriages in college towns are having unusual troubles. Her own marriage is a struggle.

Perhaps she sees others' marriages through personal gloom.

She does insist, however, that the marriages she is talking about are real—and that we need to take account of them in our theorizing about how wonderful marriage is.

Marriage is very near the heart of a Christian view of sex, so the truth of Ruth's observations is quite crucial. It is all very well to speak eloquently about the beauty of marriage. Just how beautiful are marriages in real life?

When I think about the marriages *I* know, I come up with a different view from Ruth's. I don't think many of my friends would say, except on a particularly bad night, that they wish they were married to someone else. But that doesn't mean they would jump to describe their marriages as happy. Happy? When so much time and energy goes into learning to live with each other? When so many nights one or the other of them is depressed, or angry, or uncommunicative? When the same problems that surfaced last year surface this year? An awful lot of married people I know are still grieving for their dying dreams. I would not describe most of their marriages as bad. But I would describe them as *hard.*

It is hard to be happy when one partner craves conversation and emotion while the other prefers solitude. How did two people so unlike in personality ever fall in love?

Happy? It is hard to be happy when one partner runs up credit-card bills without a shred of worry, while the other is a worrier who loses sleep every time he sees the VISA bill.

Happy? It is hard to be happy when one partner is depressed and agitated at least one day out of three, and keeps her husband awake by thrashing around in their double bed all night while grieving over lost youth or fading dreams or something—she usually only gets more agitated if you probe.

These are among the marriages I know well enough to have an idea what goes on under the surface. They are, in fact, from my list of "good" marriages. The spouses are fine people who really do love each other. They don't have what you would call "serious problems" from the three

Big A's—adultery, alcoholism or abuse. None of them, so far as I know, suffers from deep sexual inhibitions or dysfunctions. These are not what I would call bad marriages. They are merely hard.

Such marriages require compromise. They require sacrifice. A wife must, perhaps, endure her husband's moving from one job to another in a seemingly endless search for job satisfaction. A husband must, perhaps, endure his wife's deep, enduring depression, in which she tastes bitterness in everything.

Most Christians, and a good many non-Christians, would say that such compromises and sacrifices are the price you pay for a greater shared happiness. Overall, the satisfaction of married life makes it worth "working at"—even when the work is hard.

But how hard? There is a wide spectrum of troubles, from chronic messiness to chronic abusiveness. Just where does "hard" turn to "hopeless"? At what point do you say, "No more"?

When to Cry "Too Much"

People's answer to that depends a great deal on what they believe leads to happiness. Many people in our society believe happiness is an individual matter. They therefore have an easy conscience about divorce. If someone leaves a relationship but gains greater peace of mind, well and good. (There are regretful backward glances at the cost children must pay, but rarely the suggestion that an unhappy marriage should be preserved just for them.)

Conservative Christians, on the other hand, stress happiness gained through relationship—in families, in churches, in communities. Every enduring relationship requires commitment, and with that goes some sacrifice of individual freedom. Christians tend to think those sacrifices are worth it, at least in the long run.

Nonetheless, I believe most Western Christians agree with the rest of our society that happiness is the reason for marriage. We might differ from non-Christians in our assessment of the chances of happiness, or the path to achieve it, but our fundamental values don't really differ. If a marriage has no realistic chance of happiness no matter how long and well people tough it out, we wonder why it should be preserved. Maybe it should—we know what Jesus thought of divorce—but most Christians I know aren't very clear on why.

That leaves us with the problem of those hard marriages. Some of them, no doubt, will get through long rough periods and become happy. But will all become truly happy? Or to put the question more precisely, is their state the happiest they are likely to achieve—married, unmarried or married to different partners? If you're aiming at happiness, is staying married always the best way to achieve it?

I think of my friend Paul. He was divorced from his first wife ten years ago. Both were Christians, but they had been basically unhappy from the very beginning. Eventually they gave up. Paul has remarried to a wonderful, giving person who knows how to live with him and love him. She, too, had been divorced. Now, together, they both seem very happy.

Most of us can think of people like that. Not that divorce and remarriage always have such positive effects. But they certainly do sometimes, and that has to cast doubt into the minds of people struggling with hard marriages. Do they really need to struggle?

Push far enough along on the spectrum of troubles, and very few people would insist that a marriage be kept intact. Infidelity, drug addiction, mental illness, physical or sexual abuse, frigidity, homosexuality, long-term unemployment: as these and other severe problems persist, an increasing number of people would stop insisting on sacrifice. At some point the question becomes "Sacrifice for what?" Some marriages seem hopeless of ever achieving happiness.

Exalting Marriage

Their problems aren't helped by the way Christians sometimes exalt marriage. If married partners must be each other's best friends, share all of each other's interests, have ecstatic sex on a regular schedule, live in a romantic glow and at the same time save the fabric of society . . . well, the truth is that people who expect all this will often feel cheated. Marriage is an institution enabling two ordinary, lumpish people to share life together. Not many people find that heaven on earth.

And there is another, deeper problem: these idealistic conceptions almost substitute marriage for salvation. Single people get that message quite clearly in "family-oriented" churches: they are "on hold" in perpetual adolescence until they can enter (or reenter) the fullness of life—marriage.

In our current sexual and marital confusion, substituting "family" for salvation is very tempting. Many people long for security and clarity and old-fashioned values. One of the attractions of church is that it's such a family-oriented place. People would rather hear that Jesus will give them a happy marriage than that Jesus will forgive them for their sins. It's possible to worship the traditional family. That, like the idol of intimacy, is a god that will fail us.

Leaders of the Mormon church have made such "family orientation" central to their gospel. They have long repudiated Jesus' statement that there is no marriage in heaven, seeing (correctly) that he put marriage in a position of relative rather than absolute value. They, by contrast with Jesus, offer marriage and family as a little piece of heaven right here on earth. "A Parent's Guide," an official publication of the Latter-day Saints, puts it this way: "Since eternal life with our Father will be lived in family units, the ultimate goal of a man or boy is to become an effective husband and father, and the ultimate goal of a woman or girl is to become an effective wife and mother." Note the use of the word *ultimate*.

The New Testament sees life very differently. The only ultimate purpose of any human being is to be the servant of Jesus Christ, whether married or single. Jesus came into the world preaching the kingdom of God, not the family. (He warned that the kingdom would sometimes shatter families.) We know, on Jesus' authority, that our marriages will not carry on in heaven; something different and better will be there. The New Testament offers no ground whatsoever for absolutizing family life. Marriage ain't heaven—nor was it meant to be. It only points toward heaven.

The Second Story

The Old Testament tells a second universal love story: the marriage of God to his people. In this story, like the story of Adam and Eve, all people on earth can recognize themselves. But this love story, coming after the Fall, bears little resemblance to the passionate happiness of Eden. It is definitely a marriage of passion, but it is equally a marriage that can only be called "hard." It is not a happy marriage, nor does it seem that there is any earthly hope it will become one.

This will, I know, sound harsh and strange to many who are used to thinking of God's relationship to his people as a model. It *is* a model, but an extremely realistic model. It is a model of how to live in a hard relationship. The most notable characteristics of this marriage are the unfaithfulness of the bride and the passionate, tortured response of the husband. When the marriage of God to Israel is described in the Old Testament, it nearly always provokes a torrent of angry words. Take Jeremiah, for example, as he cites God's accusations against his beloved. Listen to these words as though you were overhearing angry taunts through thin apartment walls:

"I remember the devotion of your youth,
    how as a bride you loved me
and followed me through the desert. . . .
Consider then and realize
    how evil and bitter it is for you
    when you forsake the LORD your God
    and have no awe of me,"
        declares the Lord,
        the LORD Almighty. . . .
"Indeed, on every high hill
    and under every spreading tree
    you lay down as a prostitute. . . .
How can you say, 'I am not defiled? . . .'"
You are a swift she-camel
    running here and there,

a wild donkey accustomed to the desert,
    sniffing the wind in her craving—
    in her heat who can restrain her?
Any males that pursue her need not tire themselves;
    at mating time they will find her. . . .
You have lived as a prostitute with many lovers—
    would you now return to me?"
        declares the LORD. (Jeremiah 2:2, 19-20, 23-24; 3:1)

Or consider the even rougher language of Ezekiel, Jeremiah's contemporary:

> You adulterous wife! You prefer strangers to your own husband! Every prostitute receives a fee, but you give gifts to all your lovers, bribing them to come to you. . . .
>
> Therefore I am going to gather all your lovers, with whom you found pleasure, those you loved as well as those you hated. I will gather them against you from all around and will strip you in front of them, and they will see all your nakedness. . . . I will bring upon you the blood vengeance of my wrath and jealous anger. Then I will hand you over to your lovers. . . . They will strip you of your clothes and take your fine jewelry and leave you naked and bare. They will bring a mob against you, who will stone you and hack you to pieces with their swords. (Ezekiel 16:32-33, 37-40)

Yet these terrible words—and they are typical of many in the prophets—are interlaced with pleading love:

"Return, faithless Israel,"
    declares the LORD,
    "I will frown on you no longer,
for I am merciful," declares the LORD,
    "I will not be angry forever.
Only acknowledge your guilt. . . .
Return, faithless people," declares the LORD, "for I am your husband."
(Jeremiah 3:12-14)

The fury of God toward his bride is dreadful. He is not going to live meekly with her infidelity. He cannot. He loves her too much, and he has too much self-respect. He will never be content with a bad marriage; he will rage against it until it is changed.

This ought to do away with any simplistic application of Philippians 2 to marriage. Many wives have been told that the godly approach to an unfaithful or abusive partner is quiet patience. Sometimes they can only pray, hope and endure, it is said.

God is no model of that. Is he quietly patient while his partner abuses his love? About as much as a tornado is a gentle wind. God is not waiting for Israel to see the error of her ways, to be convinced by his Christian love. God demands what he deserves.

A wife who did the same might be accused, by some Christians, of selfishness. And in some cases they would be right. Some marital counseling urges an abused partner to stop worrying about her partner but simply to "take care of herself." That, however, is not what God is doing when he demands what he deserves. If God only worried about himself, he would forget Israel utterly. He doesn't "need" Israel. But God loves Israel. Through Israel, furthermore, he wants to redeem the world. Therefore he demands that their marriage become what it was meant to be. To the extent that patience is called for, he is patient. To the extent that his anger may rock Israel from apathy, he is wildly expressive of his angry demands. Sometimes he initiates a kind of separation, letting Israel experience the result of her own choices. Yet his goal is not in doubt: he will never settle for a bad marriage. Nor can he ever give up. He must have a marriage of love and righteousness.

You cannot help but see, if you consider the whole Bible, that God's humility ultimately dominates. He threatens, blusters, shouts, punishes, he even sends his bride off into exile—but in the end he always goes and brings her back. At any sign of genuine repentance, he throws his arms open to her.

Hope persistently rises in the background—hope that God's love will someday triumph over his wife's indifference. "As a bridegroom rejoices over his bride, so will your God rejoice over you" (Isaiah 62:5).

The last word of this love story came in Jesus, who laid aside magisterial power—the power of a husband in patriarchal Israel—and submitted to his wife's rejection. She deserved to die—that was the penalty for adultery—and at the very least she deserved divorce, but he courted her lovingly. He wept for her. These are the words of a lover: "O Jerusalem, Jerusalem, you who kill the prophets and stone those sent to you, how often I have longed to gather your children together, as a hen gathers her chicks under her wings, but you were not willing" (Matthew 23:37). He finally died at her hands. Through this sacrificial act he cleansed her, so that in the end he will gain her again as a radiant bride, unstained by her past (Ephesians 2:26-27; Revelation 21:2). The prophets' hopeful vision is fulfilled in Jesus.

As Andrew Greeley writes, "The most obvious proof that one does not lose masculinity or strength by exposing one's needs and desires is to be found in Yahweh's making it quite clear how desperately he wants to be loved by his people, and making it clear indeed in explicitly sexual language. If Yahweh can admit that he 'needs' the affection of his beloved, then why should any man be afraid to admit the same thing?" And, Greeley notes, though "making demands" runs against what we have been taught love is, God is clearly a lover unafraid to make demands. "In fact, a love that is not passionate enough to demand the best from the other is not love at all."[1] Love in a hard marriage, if God is a model, is passionate, insistent, aggressive love.

Yet it is also, ultimately, love that will not let go—love that will sacrifice its own life in order to make the marriage into what it was meant to be.

Lessons

What do we learn from these two love stories? I could make almost endless lists of abstract lessons. Yet stories, I think, are most profitably used in another way—as mirrors for seeing ourselves.

We are meant to see ourselves in Adam and Eve. I can remember thinking, as an adolescent, that if I ever had a lover's body to hold through the night, I would wake each day in a glow of wonder. Such longing is the reason we marry. Yet how quickly we forget. How quickly we slump into uncommunicative, unappreciative bad moods. The story of Eden reminds us why we marry. It calls us back to our original hope and delight. It is a love story—your love story, mine—to reawaken longing.

We see ourselves in God and Israel, too. Our marriages may be made in Eden, but they do not stay there. They are cast out into the world. They are filled with jealousy, anger, frustration. Why? How is it that two people who once could barely stand to be apart sometimes can barely stand to be together? The only credible answer is the one told in Genesis's story. Wanting to be gods, we have lost our place in Eden.

If you are in a marriage like Israel's, what can give you hope? Is there any possibility that the unashamed nakedness and passionate delight of Eden can be restored? Can this love story have a happy ending? Let us look in the mirror of God and Israel. God perseveres in spite of the pain of rejection. Furthermore, he does not merely "hang in there." He perseveres in hope.

Maybe that hope is irrational. What, after all, would a marriage counselor say to God if he came in for an appointment? Can this marriage be saved? From a human point of view, no. But that is precisely why we need the mirror of this story. It tells us that something more than a human point of view is involved in love stories. Somehow, God will make his marriage like the original in Eden, and even better. He wants to save marriages—"save" in the full biblical sense of the word, not merely to preserve from divorce, but to make whole again.

To believe in this possibility takes faith. It is not for the irreligious. That is one reason to tell the story of God and his love for Israel. Stories can excite faith. Stories can inspire. Love stories can get behind our defenses and call our hearts toward what we were meant to be. We were meant to be lovers like Adam and Eve—passionate, unashamed. We were meant to be lovers like God—passionate, persistent even in pain.

When we listen to these stories, we approach marriage in a very different way from the pragmatic secularism of our age. We stop calculating how we can make ourselves happy. We begin seeking to reflect God.

St. John of the Cross wrote that love consists "not in feeling great things, but in suffering for the beloved."[2] Paul told husbands to love their wives as Christ loved the church, and Christ's love found its greatest expression on the cross. For many of us, hard marriages—our own or others'—are the closest we ever come to understanding God's stubborn, passionate love.

Marriages like these are not happiness, nor are they peace. But they are certainly a sign. Their persistence points beyond themselves. It points to God. We are loved that way by our Lord. He may not be happy with his marriage to us. But he is not about to quit.

When two people in a hard marriage stick it out, persisting and insisting that their marriage become what it was meant to be, they may or may not end up happy. They will certainly end up showing the world a sign of faith.

The Possibility of Divorce
Is there, then, no possibility of divorce? I grew up in an era when Christians didn't divorce, and I have had a hard time accepting it as Christian friends, for reasons good and bad, have lost their marriages. I have come to accept, however, that there is such a thing as a dead marriage which we do not have the power to revive, and that it is not sensible or possible to live indefinitely with a corpse. I believe with all my heart that any marriage can survive if both partners are willing to try, but I also know that sometimes one or the other simply cannot or will not struggle any longer. Jesus said that the law of Moses permitted divorce because of the hardness of people's hearts; and people's hearts have not grown any softer since Moses. Sometimes hardened hearts are an inescapable reality.

"In the beginning it was not so," Jesus told the Pharisees when they asked about divorce. Indeed, it is impossible to imagine divorce in Eden. God joins the two in delight—what could separate them? At best, divorce is an accommodation to the "hardness of heart" that has invaded Eden and forced us out. It was not meant to be so.

It was not meant to be so, but it is so. Partners abuse each other. Hearts are hardened. Marriages are destroyed. People lose hope. These are realities of human life. Christians differ in their thinking about how to respond to these facts. Some reject any compromise with defeat. They will never accept divorce. Others, myself included, will choose to accommodate the realities of failed marriages, out of pity for the people involved. Reluctantly, sadly, they will accept that the marriage is dead and cannot be revived.

Nevertheless, I also know very intimately people who have been willing to struggle and suffer and persevere through astonishing difficulties for years. They are better for it. And I am better for it. And the world is better for it, because it makes the sign of Christ.

Love That Will Not Let Go

Ruth, with whom I began this chapter, has been married for almost twenty years, and I have known her well through most of those. They have not been easy years. She and her husband are both intense, dedicated, complicated. What causes their troubles? Sex, for one. They often can't get their signals straight, and feelings are hurt over imaginary (or maybe real) rejections. They compete with each other. They hold grudges. But maybe greater than any other single problem is this slippery one: neither one of them knows how to encourage the other. They try, but their attempts are always prickly. When one makes an effort, the other often rebuffs it. You could spend a long time analyzing why, and maybe you would figure it out. But how they are supposed to change is a different matter.

They have gone to counseling, and they have found some other couples with whom to share a genuine and deep fellowship. I've watched and tried to encourage their attempts. Sometimes their marriage really has seemed to be better. Other times, it has slipped back into grudges and embittered silences.

If the purpose of marriage were purely to provide happy intimacy, their marriage might have been called purposeless. Oh, sure, it's quite possible they would have been as troubled with other partners, or alone. But I suspect they would have taken their chances. They have stayed married largely because they were brought up to believe that marriage is for life, and that divorce is wrong. Also, I suppose, because they are stubborn people. They don't give up easily. They keep on trying.

And one more factor: they really do love each other. In their own tormented way, they do need each other. Their own personal legacy of Eden is not entirely used up.

Not long ago, when I was out to dinner with them both, Ruth looked at me and said she had an announcement to make. "Robert and I have been talking about our marriage, and . . . well . . . we think we have grown out of most of our problems." Tears came to my eyes, because I understood what lay behind her typical understatement. She is painfully honest in all she claims, and she wasn't claiming bliss. She was claiming that the struggle had, finally, led somewhere. They were glad to be married. The marriage was being saved.

For days, even weeks, I carried their happiness around with me, like a little ball of sunlight. As a friend I had suffered with them; now I was so glad to share their relief. I have never known anyone who struggled harder to make a marriage prevail over its difficulties, and it filled me with hope that they had at last seen success.

I will be very glad if I get to see them enjoy the kind of love that Eden knew: relaxed, joyful, passionate. I am very grateful, too, that I have been able to see their persistent love, love such as God showed to Israel. Such long-suffering love is a sign that has pointed me to something beyond myself. Fidelity in a hard marriage is a sign pointing to the long-suffering faithfulness of God himself.

Our society now treats divorce as an ordinary happenstance, like a car breaking down. These things happen; it's too bad. You try your best but sometimes it doesn't work out. But for Christians, divorce should be a failure and an aberration from Eden in each and every case. It is always a cause for mourning, not merely because of the personal distress the broken marriage has caused but because divorce communicates something to the world. It says the partners in the marriage have lost hope, lost faith, lost love, and have quit at something God ordained. People will quit, in a fallen world, and in some way or another we will have to recognize that. But let us not call it anything other than what it is. It is a failure to make the sign of God's kingdom.

When God, angry at his people, threatened to destroy them and start over, Moses remonstrated with him: "Then the Egyptians will hear about it! . . . And they will tell the inhabitants of this land about it. . . . If you put these people to death all at one time, the nations who have heard this report about you will say, 'The LORD was not able to bring these people into the land he promised them' " (Numbers 14:13-16).

God had every justification to divorce his people. He could not do so, however, without damaging his reputation. Once he had started the marriage, his honor demanded that he finish it. So it is with human marriages. God joins the two together. His honor as well as ours is at stake. "What God has joined together, let man not separate." When we do separate them, we give up on God's purposes for them. We make an antisign of God's kingdom. It is a sign of Humpty Dumpty, of unredeemable brokenness.

Institutions or Individuals?

A man comes to see a marriage counselor. He has been married for twelve years, and he says that all twelve have been unhappy. During the entire twelve years the two have never successfully had intercourse. His wife has vaginismus, a condition that makes intercourse very painful. They have been to counseling together, but it has not helped. He and his wife are committed Christians; the wife does not want a divorce. The husband, however, is ready to quit. He knows that marriage is important, but he says, "I don't believe that God would destroy two individuals in order to preserve an institution."

Put that way, who could disagree? God loves people, not institutions. To anyone who feels for this man and his wife, divorce will seem to be an act of liberating kindness. The twelve-year stalemate will be broken. Finally, some relief from the misery! Two individuals will be rescued from an institution that has become a prison. The marriage is a failure; divorce will seem to be a limited triumph—like a successful retreat from a lost battle.

When one thinks more carefully, however, questions arise. They will leave one prison—but will they enter another? Their marriage has been miserable because they both suffer from miserable personal problems. Will the net sum of misery decrease because they have gone their own ways? Or will it be compounded by isolation and loneliness as they are separate? Initially divorce will feel like an improvement, but will it remain so?

Another question: why have they not had intercourse in twelve years? Vaginismus is treatable. They have been to marriage counseling, but have they really explored all possibilities for healing? Or have they merely made a gesture at getting help, so that forever after they could say, "We tried"?

These quibbles are practical ones. Extended from these two individuals to our whole society, this line of thinking would ask, "Have increased divorces made people happier?" No one can answer this question precisely, because happiness cannot be measured. However, there is reason to think that a divorce-happy society is not happier.

But suppose that all practical questions are answered. The man's question remains. Would God destroy two individuals in order to preserve an institution? Of course not. But what do you mean by *destroy?*

A Christian would have to conclude that destroying a person involves more than disturbing his health or peace of mind. You want to destroy a person? Cut him off from the possibility of meaning. Let him do exactly as he wants—lie by the pool all day reading *People* or *Hello,* or play the stock market for millions—but let his life mean nothing to his family or friends, or even to himself.

There have been, obviously, many who suffered (as martyrs, in the extreme case) believing that while suffering they were living at the peak of their existence. Is it possible to suffer in the same way for marriage? Is it possible that the command "Husbands, love your wives, just as Christ loved the church and gave himself up for her" applies precisely here?

Thinking of this man in terms of our two primary stories is revealing. He was created to live Adam's story, passionately responding to his wife in joy. But perhaps hardness of heart has destroyed that possibility. If so, what can he do? He can divorce, making the Humpty Dumpty sign. It would be hard to blame him; none of us would want to be in his place. But there is another possibility. He can carry on God's story, refusing to accept a bad marriage, but refusing to give up on it either.

Why should he persist? Because it will surely make him happy? Because it will preserve an important institution? No, because it will allow him the privilege of making the sign of God's kingdom. He will show his faith in the possibilities of God's redeeming that which he has joined together.

God's story, we must remember, is not ultimately sad. It is not a matter of hanging on without hope. It is a story in which love triumphs in the end. However, in order for the story to end that way, Jesus had to die undeservingly. We, as his disciples, have been called to share in such sufferings. Surely we cannot exempt marriage from that call. Surely in marriage as in all of life Jesus's words ring true: "Whoever loses his life for my sake will find it" (Matthew 10:39).

9
THE
BOUNDARIES
AROUND LOVE

Most Westerners agree that a happy marriage is a beautiful thing. They may even applaud an enduring, hard marriage. It's the Christian rules they can't stand, especially the strict rules against sex outside marriage.

Take James. His life is a mess. Two weeks ago his third wife, Judy, moved to another state with a woman she met at a seminar on inner illumination. "My life is just a country-western song," he says, and thinks that's some kind of original line.

He doesn't really care who knows. He'll talk about it to anybody. One time, though, he was pouring out his story to someone he'd met on the train going into the city. The guy began talking about his church and invited James to attend.

"That's one place I'll never go, no matter how far down I get," James swears fervently. "Religion is just a big guilt trip. I don't need their guilt. I don't need their rules."

He is far from alone. Sometimes it appears only one serious sin is left in America: narrow-mindedness. Every other wrongdoing can be understood, accepted, psychologized, therapized. But there is no excuse for considering other people sinners.

This puts Christians in a difficult position. We cannot hide the unmistakable scriptural prominence of rules.

Certainly, rules are not the heart of our message. Our message is the good news of salvation, not the law.

Certainly, too, sin goes deeper than rules. Sin is a condition of the whole person. Someone may be outwardly flawless yet inwardly rotten. This was Jesus' chief criticism of the Pharisees: they had failed to understand how deep and intractable sin is. By defining it superficially, they had managed to make themselves look good.

The rules cannot give life. They never saved anyone. In the sexual realm, obeying the rules will not guarantee a faithful marriage or a fruitful single life. Rules are inherently superficial. Yet rules are part of the Christian witness about sexuality. The law—which certainly includes rules—is a teacher and a guide toward salvation. The good news without the law's requirements becomes merely cheap grace.

Setting Some Standards

Some people would admit that some kinds of sexual standards are necessary, but they hate to see these standards rigidly codified. That, they say, goes against the very nature of good and loving sexuality. Sex should be spontaneous and emotive. Let us honor principles such as love, care and communication, they say, but not a rigid code.

James Nelson is perhaps the most influential American theologian who holds this position: "Sexual sin is alienation from our sexuality; harmful ideas and acts arise out of this. When I become alienated from my body and my sexuality, I will tend to see the world as though everything involves an either/or conflict. Everything will be either good or bad, right or wrong, gay or straight, me or them."[1] Nelson would like us to be more flexible in our evaluations, looking at what people mean by their actions and taking into account the entire picture of their lives. And he goes further: he says that the desire to categorize actions as right or wrong is itself a symptom of sinfulness, which he defines as alienation from our sexuality. He seems to be thinking of stereotypical "old maids": people so uncomfortable with their bodies they don't like paying attention to subtleties and inner meanings in sexual deeds. It's easier to just condemn it all as sin.

There's something to this stereotype. Andrew Greeley is surely right in claiming, "The legalism of the past . . . assume[s] that the problems of sexuality can be solved in terms of whom you sleep with and what particular organs are combined in what ways."[2]

That form of legalism is dead wrong. Sex can be "proper" without being at all "right." Every marriage counselor sees couples who have never committed adultery, but whose relationship seethes with anger, frustration and bitterness. It is *not* enough that married couples be faithful to each other, if faithfulness merely means staying out of bed with other people.

However, staying out of other people's beds is not a bad place to start toward more positive forms of faithfulness.

Two Kinds of Standards

There are two kinds of standards. The most important are positive callings. "Love the Lord your God with all your heart and with all your soul and with all your strength and with all your mind" is the greatest commandment, though there is a great deal of fuzziness in applying it and no "penalty" for disobedience. The same could be said of "Honor your father and your mother." Such commands set an ideal. They confront us, they teach us, they rebuke us, but they have a shortcoming: they can easily be evaded by someone who imagines him or herself to be good and does not want to be contradicted.

Another kind of rule is more definite, and usually negative. These are the rules that people object to. "You shall not steal." "You shall not murder." "You shall not give false testimony against your neighbor." "You shall not make for yourself an idol." "You shall not commit adultery." Such standards are "yes and no," "right or wrong." Nelson suggests that those alienated from the body will like such commands. The truth is nearer the opposite. These are commands suited to the body.

One great advantage of the body is its definiteness. It either does or does not do a certain act. For Nelson sexual acts are a form of communication; their meaning depends on what you have in mind. But the physical body sets limits on such flexibility. Theft is theft regardless of motive; someone else's bed is never to be confused with my bed, no matter how I yearned for wholeness while I was there.

Real morality requires both kinds of command. Rules cannot probe the heart; they can keep you out of the wrong bed, but they can't teach you how to make love in your own. Today, though, we live in a society that would like very much to retain only the positive commands—only to speak of meaningful relationships and love and wholeness. This is really an attempt to escape—to escape responsibility for our actions, to escape the body and its definiteness. We would like never to be "judged." We would like to be only what we imagine ourselves to be. The negative commands force us to confront the truth about ourselves.

A group of Christians, for example, builds a very powerful ideology of victory over sin. They are elated with their certainty that God has given them power over evil—until one of their leaders is caught in adultery, or with his hand in the till. Then there is no escaping the factuality of the sin—he did it with his body. Evidently that Christian group has not yet cornered the Holy Spirit. No doubt they had sinned against the positive standards a thousand times. But it was the negative standard—the rule— that caught their attention.

To avoid such "right or wrong" morality is to evade the truth about ourselves, and to evade responsibility for repairing our wrongs. That's the case with James. He doesn't like rules because he doesn't want to think too hard about his life. The world is filled with people like James today. Much is wrong—AIDS, abortions, teenage pregnancies, broken families—and the victims are everywhere. But who is responsible? No one, but no one, comes forward to say "me."

No Adultery

The Bible's primary rule on sexuality is this: no adultery allowed. The rule is intended to protect marriage. It does nothing to ensure that the marriage will be good. It is merely a strong wall, protecting a married couple from an alien and evil force that can destroy any marriage, good or bad. When you go outside this wall, it says, you may never come back in one piece.

All marriages begin with the same response that Adam made to Eve: passionate recognition of each other. "This is now bone of my bones and flesh of my flesh." This leads, instinctively, to an exclusive bond. Lovers say: "Let us be together always. Let no one else come between us." And they ask, even if silently, for guarantees: "You will never leave me, will you? There cannot be someone else?"

Marriage, you might say, is an instinctive institution. Exclusivity and permanence are reflexes of love. D. H. Lawrence—no Christian, certainly—wrote, "The instinct of fidelity is perhaps the deepest instinct in the great complex we call sex. Where there is real sex there is the underlying passion for fidelity."[3]

But—here is the problem—these reflexes do not stay. Passion cools; it cannot sustain itself without some outside help—and this help comes from our marriage vows. In Christian vows, we promise to love and receive love until death. We promise to give our all to one lover, for life. This is where the rule against adultery comes in. It is a practical marker, testing whether we have really lived our vows. Have we persisted in love? If we have been sleeping with someone else, we surely have not.

Bad Sex Drives Out the Good

Of course, some think the positive vows should be enough. If a couple tries hard to love each other, won't they succeed in "affair-proofing" their relationship?

To Maggie Scarf, an affair is virtual proof that something is lacking in the marriage. "The affair's very existence . . . indicate[s] that the intimacy in the couple's emotional system is out of balance. Someone is frightened about getting too close, or someone is overly frustrated—hungering for an intimacy that is lacking."[4] She assumes that partners in a good relationship won't be tempted by adultery. Good sex will drive out the bad.

Yet reality is often just the opposite: bad sex drives out the good. No one seems invulnerable to sexual temptation, and an affair, however "meaningless," has the potential to ruin even the best marriage. Paul Pearsall, though he advertises the superiority of "super marital sex," comments that "one of the saddest paradoxes among the thousand couples [studied] was the fact that the persons you would assume to be the best of all spouses sometimes became involved outside the marriage. If not actually interacting sexually, they were at least flirting with the possibility." He suggests that this is because an attractive marriage partner will be attractive to others outside the marriage as well. The "best partners" suffer the worst temptations.[5]

A mere decade ago, popular books claimed that an occasional affair could spice up a relationship. Now, thanks to the cruel instructions of experience, "open marriages" are understood to be those with the bottom falling out. Adultery has devastating consequences. Scarf describes a woman who had discovered her husband's infidelity: She "found herself standing in the middle of a department store with no idea why she had gone there or what she had intended to purchase. 'I felt as if the very floor I stood on was moving, waving, and buckling underneath me. It was as if I myself and the world around me were completely unreal.' "[6]

Philip Blumstein and Pepper Schwartz, in their sociological study *American Couples: Money, Work, Sex,* found that "husbands and wives who had had extramarital sex were more likely to break up, whether it happened at the beginning of the marriage or after many years." Their comments are revealing:

> It is widely believed that with a truly happy relationship, partners would not be "driven" to non-monogamy. Another piece of folk wisdom is that partners go outside for sex when there is too little of it at home. We find that heterosexual couples who are monogamous [that is, who don't commit adultery] have neither more nor less sex than those who are not. . . . Monogamous and non-monogamous heterosexual men and women are on average equally pleased with their sex lives together. Another possibility exists: that partners are non-monogamous because they are fundamentally unhappy with the relationship. There is no evidence for this contention. Heterosexuals who have non-monogamous sex are on average as happy with their relationships as monogamous people. But they are *not* as certain that their relationships will last. . . . For most heterosexuals, non-monogamy is associated with less commitment to a future together.[7]

Taking a positive vow of commitment and internalizing the negative rule against adultery are two sides of the same coin.

Blumstein and Schwartz also collected data on couples who were living together. Eighteen months after their initial interview, such "cohabitors" were between two and four times more likely than married couples to have dissolved their relationship. (Gay and lesbian couples were even less stable.) And not coincidentally, the chances of affairs in a cohabiting couple were nearly twice as great. (Gay and lesbian couples were even more prone to affairs.) The lack of commitment and the potential for affairs went together—as did the likelihood of breaking apart.[8]

A partner's infidelity is more than just a disappointing choice to prefer another person (for a night, or longer); it is a stab in the gut. It threatens any relationship, regardless of how loving. It is an action that cannot be mediated by good intentions. It betrays the partner who has entrusted life, body and soul, to another. It makes him or her into a sexual competitor.

Is there any such thing as a meaningless fling? The apostle Paul, in his comments about the inevitable unity that sex brings, even with a prostitute

(1 Corinthians 6:16), would deny it. So would the vast majority of people, if they were talking about their own spouse's infidelity. Blumstein and Schwartz tried to differentiate between a meaningful affair and a meaningless fling. But the people they asked made little of the distinction. Among wives, for example, 93 percent were threatened by a meaningful affair by their husbands, and 84 percent by a meaningless fling. For husbands the distinction was even smaller. Only among gay couples was there a widespread belief that meaningless sex was a possibility.[9]

Marriage demands, positively, that we make a pledge to love for life. Negatively, it demands that we abhor adultery. To brush aside that rule, emphasizing the positive pledge without the negative command, is to kid yourself. Adultery destroys the possibility of Eden.

We cannot build strong marriages without fighting hard against adultery. We will have to preach against it, and discipline those who disobey the command. If this makes us seem harsh and rule-bound, then that is the public relations problem we will have to contend with. Far better that image problem than the reality of broken marriages. A community that tolerates or ignores the problem of adultery is a community that has not faced the marriage-breaking realities of a sinful world.

10
PREMARITAL SEX

T he second sexual rule of the Christian church, after the rule against adultery, is the rule against premarital sex. Why is premarital sex wrong? And is it wrong in all situations?

Consider Richard and Janis, who met at their church's high-school youth group. On their first date they shared their philosophies of life, which included their feeling that they wanted to wait until marriage to have sex. Three months into their relationship, Richard told Janis that he loved her. Janis said she loved him too, and stayed up until three in the morning writing in her diary. She thought that someday she would want a record of this day of days.

Six months into their relationship, after a miniature-golf date, they went beyond kissing in the car and began to caress each other's bodies passionately, hungrily. They were both surprised to find that they didn't feel at all guilty. The next day, though, they talked it over and decided that it wasn't right for them to be petting.

Yet they did it, week after week. They tried and failed to stop. Soon they didn't care about stopping, except occasionally when they "got the guilts," as they put it. One night Richard asked Janis whether she had ever thought of making love with him. She said she thought of it all the time. For several weeks they talked it over. It seemed they would have to either break up or make love—the middle ground was too difficult. And neither one of them could remember, no matter how hard he or she tried, just what was wrong with it.

Richard and Janis are very typical of high-school lovers. They are not promiscuous. They act as though they're already married, which indeed they have vague plans someday to be. They feel tremendous love for each other, love that is something more than infatuation, since they have spent so many hours together and know each other so well. They're still teenagers, still dependent on their parents, but they have experienced considerable independence in school and in summer and part-time jobs.

Both of them intended to wait for marriage, and they still hold marriage in high esteem. It's not practical for them to think about marrying now. But if it worked out that they eventually could marry, that would be wonderful, they both think. The problem is right now. It is very hard for them to be together so much, and love each other so deeply, and yet not have intercourse.

Why should they not? On a practical level there are several reasons, particularly pregnancy and sexually transmitted disease. However, Janis and Richard could use birth control (though if they did they would be atypical high-school lovers). Assuming that they are both telling the truth about their virginity, disease should not be an issue for them. These practical concerns are significant, but not absolute.

Superficially, sexual intercourse between two such students may have "nothing wrong with it." That is, they may experience no obvious harm— no suffocating guilt or evident psychological damage. According to most studies, at least half of American high-school students engage in sexual intercourse by the time they graduate, and of these, most continue to be sexually active up until the time they marry, usually sometime in their twenties. A great many will have problems as a result, but not all of them will. Richard and Janis have plenty of friends who are sexually involved, and it doesn't seem to have ruined their lives.

Janis and Richard are not guilty of adultery—neither is married. They are not violating their own or others' marital vows. What is wrong with what they want to do? The question is acute in our culture, where marriages are delayed until ten years or more after puberty. Some would argue that expecting chastity under such conditions is sheer fantasy. Others would argue that trying to enforce chastity leads to all kinds of psychological trauma and antisocial behavior.

Divorced people and single adults pose a related question. They are presumably mature enough to deal with the risks of a sexual relationship. Why should they be deprived of sex?

I have already dealt with many of the practical results of premarital sex in the first chapter of this book. For society as a whole, and for vulnerable people in particular, it is disastrous. Here, though, I want to deal with the problem on an individual level. After all, if the biblical prohibition of *porneia*[1] applies at all, it is a claim on each individual, no matter how mature and strong he or she may be. The law is aimed at society, but no less at the individual, whom it should train in righteousness. What is so "right" about avoiding premarital sex?

Another way of asking that question is, What is protected within the boundary against "fornication"? Two ways of life: marriage and celibacy.

Protecting the Future

Richard and Janis will probably someday want to marry. Yet marriage is a difficult task. We want Janis and Richard, if at all possible, to marry successfully.

The logic of the law against *porneia* is that the best marriages are formed where two people come together sexually only with each other, within the bounds of marriage. They both enter their first marriage as virgins.

Why so? Why should sex before marriage have anything to do with sex after marriage? Why should sex with one partner have any carryover effect on sex with another partner? The answer lies in Paul's exegesis of "one flesh" in 1 Corinthians 6:12-20. According to Paul, something happens when two people come together sexually, something independent of their intentions or their state of mind. Sex has its own meaning. That meaning stays with you, even after you have forgotten the particulars of the sexual act (as someone may, after enough partners, quite forget how many he or she has been with).

What is this meaning? "Do you not know that he who unites himself with a prostitute is one with her in body?" The meaning is that you become "one" with a person who is not properly yours. You penetrate each other. That interpenetration stays with you. That *person* stays with you. If there is only one partner, the specific personality and body will stay with you. If there are many, there will be a fairly faceless crowd with you. But whether one face or a crowd of faces, they will be with you. If and when you marry, they will, in a sense, "meet" your spouse. Your spouse will want to know about them (or if not, will sacrifice the intimacy of knowing an important aspect of your life). Your spouse will experience them, because your spirit and body have been shaped by them.

Paul is saying that a person who has had sex is different from someone who has not had sex. He is also saying, undoubtedly, that someone who has had sex with two people is different from someone who has had sex with one person. Further, he is saying that someone who has had sex under proper circumstances—within marriage—will be affected differently from a person who has had sex under improper circumstances.

Paul makes no mention of virginity. (The Bible does not often mention it, though in Old Testament Israel a woman was supposed to be able to demonstrate to her husband that she was virginal—see Deuteronomy 22.) Yet Paul's logic may be easier to understand if we apply it specifically to virginity. Virgins ought to be different from nonvirgins, by Paul's logic.

So it has been thought, in all advanced societies, where virginity was valued at least in women. Today the value of virginity is disallowed, mainly out of reaction against the double standard. We have eliminated the double standard by letting women be as promiscuous as men, rather than by insisting that men be as faithful as women. It is believed today that virginity means nothing but an orifice penetrated or unpenetrated.

The First Time

Yet the cult of "the first time" suggests that people still know that virginity makes a difference. A much-reviewed book collected stories from dozens of celebrities of their "first time." Movies frequently celebrate an adolescent's "first time." It is supposed to be a very important initiation.

Imagine how those same movies would portray a thirty-five-year-old who had remained a virgin. In the movies, such a person would be hopeless—until he or she lost his virginity. In the contemporary sense, a virgin is different all right—badly so. A virgin doesn't know what it's all about. A virgin is naive, "out of it," unformed, inexperienced.

For our culture, those qualities are bad. For Paul they would undoubtedly be good. It is good for unmarried people to be sexually unformed. A virgin is inexperienced, and that makes him or her radically open to being formed by "the first time" with a husband or wife. A virgin is ready to bond firmly to another person. A nonvirgin has already made, and broken, at least one bond, which makes the second bond harder to form.

A woman who has been with other men, or a man who has been with other women, will always be able to compare—compare the beauty of bodies, compare the varieties of sexual technique. The other bodies stay with you, when you have known them that way. Yet comparisons are deathly to love. The person who marries as a virgin will be incapable of comparisons.

Virgins have a kind of shyness of body, because their bodies have been given to no one. The shyness may be nothing more than shyness. But it can also be a sign that the body is highly valued, a gift to be presented to one person only. Someone who marries as a virgin will have a singular vision of marriage, not as the best possible option among other sexual liaisons, but as the only one. As monotheists are bid to bow to one God only, so a virgin enters marriage to be joined to one person only, forever. A marriage formed this way has a different quality from one in which both partners have been joined to other bodies.

Advice for the Sexually Experienced

Very well, someone says. That may be good for virgins, but very few adults today are virgins. They have had sexual experiences in high school and college and beyond. Or they have been married and are now divorced. What is the value for them in staying away from sex after all that?

Furthermore, don't you make widows into second-rate partners? They aren't going to become virgins again.

Perhaps this is why the Bible makes little of virginity. When Paul wrote warning the Corinthians away from prostitutes, he did not specify that his instructions were for virgins. Indeed, there probably weren't many in Corinth. Paul has a positive command as well as a negative one. Both apply to the sexually experienced. He says not only to "flee from sexual immorality" but also to "honor God with your body" (1 Corinthians 6:18, 20).

That is precisely what a widow has presumably done. In her marriage, in bed, she has honored God. Her nonvirginity may represent a positive sexual achievement, rather than a negative one. So for Paul she is not a second-rate partner at all. Her sexual experiences have formed her in a good way, rather than in a way that dishonors God.

But what about those who have lost count of their extramarital liaisons? What difference could one more make to a person who has known many? A virgin is different from a nonvirgin. But how different is a man who has known five women from a man who has known six?

The difference may not be in the number of past partners, but in whether the man has stopped adding more—or has not stopped. That would make, at any rate, a difference in his relationship to God. Those who continue to pursue unmarried sex decide not to honor God with their body. They refuse to use their sexuality for the purpose it was intended. If their excuse is "it's too late for me," it is because they refuse to believe themselves forgiven and renewed in the image of God. They refuse to believe that God can change the likes of them.

Paul urged the Corinthians not to be united to prostitutes because he wanted them to live in unity with the Lord. He clearly thought that unless they stopped *porneia*, they would be incapable of honoring God with their bodies.

The question of sex outside of marriage is often put this way: "Why deprive them?" One must ask, Deprive them of what? Of sex? But of what kind of sex, if it is outside of marriage? Do we deprive them of sex as a compulsive need? Sex as an abuse of themselves and others? Sex as a depersonalized, short-term round of biological stimulation? Sex as an opportunity to make their bodies known to others, and then to have them compared and rejected?

For unmarried people too, bad sex drives out the good. It is easy to see this in the current singles scene, in which the chief complaint seems to be (from women, particularly) that all the good partners are already taken, and that men won't commit themselves. When easy sex is available, many do not wait and work for sex within a strong marriage. Commitments become a rarity, because people don't need them to gain sexual pleasure. By not depriving single people of bad sex, we may end up depriving them of good sex.

Why deprive them? A Christian will answer this question in another way as well. Modern people assume that life without sex is always deprived. That is not an assumption Christians can make, since our Lord himself was celibate. In at least one case celibacy was the very opposite of deprivation. His was the richest life ever known.

The Critical Difference of Commitment

Janis and Richard, no matter how much they love each other, cannot be sure that they will stay together. Statistically the likelihood of teenagers' staying together for even a year is very small. Janis and Richard love each other, but theirs is not a fully ripened love. It is, in fact, little more than a seed. God wants them to grow a love that will last until death. Perhaps they will, but there is nothing like certainty that their love amounts to that. More likely, it is merely an intense teenage love affair. It is not ready to bear the weight of sex.

Of course, Richard and Janis may someday marry. We can hope they will, but even if they did that would hardly justify sexual relations now. Premarital sex makes a poor preparation for marriage. Paul Pearsall notes that in the one thousand couples he studied, "the large majority of their problems originated during the bonding phase of their relationship.

"Typically, the sexual interaction was male-instigated and female-dictated. . . . There was little verbal communication during the sex of courtship, and the women reported rare or inconsistent orgasmic experience. . . . Couples fell into bad habits, rushing sex, using it for negotiation, feeling guilty, trying to sneak to have sex and all, and sometimes cheating on a partner for sex while staying with the courting partner for a relationship." Pearsall concludes, "Sexual intercourse between men and women is constructive only within marriage." He adds, "It is interesting to note that Masters and Johnson and other sex therapists almost always tell their couples in treatment to stop having intercourse, to become reacquainted on deeper and broader personal levels before moving on to the intimacy of sexual intercourse. I suggest that we use this recommendation for our courtship patterns as well. A little preventative sex therapy couldn't hurt."[2]

What Difference Does a Piece of Paper Make?
Let me distinguish between three levels of premarital sex: recreational, experimental and preceremonial.

Recreational sex is sex devoid of commitment. The two individuals come together for the pleasure of it. They may be open to a permanent bond, but that is far from the front of their minds. They enjoy each other for the moment. Paul was talking about recreational sex when he wrote to the Corinthians.

Experimental sex also has no commitment, but it is interested in commitment. This is the most common form of premarital sex today. The two partners aren't mainly seeking temporary pleasure; they are after long-term love. However, they are not yet willing or able to commit themselves to each other.

Along with the Richards and Janises of the world, most couples who are living together fit this description. For them, "living together" is a trial. They want to see how it feels to share life. Very, very few "living together" couples stay in that state indefinitely. (Blumstein and Schwartz were unable to locate enough "cohabitors" who had been together ten years or more to make a statistical sample.) Either they marry or they split. The majority split.

Studies demonstrate that experimental sex doesn't work. Couples who lived together before marriage are more prone to divorce, not less. They don't learn whether or not they're compatible—they learn how to treat each other lightly.

It's a moot point, anyway. Trial marriages are only useful if, as in many cases, the trial fails—you find through living together that you aren't suited for each other. Presumably, you can then walk away unscathed. But the apostle Paul would say you can't walk away unscathed. Paul would say that experimenting with sex is like experimenting with pregnancy. Sex always creates a unity between two people, a unity that has lasting effects. Experimental sex may be morally better than recreational sex. But it is never good enough.

Preceremonial sex is between two people who believe they are committed. They intend to marry. They may simply get carried away before the wedding day. Or they may consider the actual ceremony a technicality. Once they have committed themselves to each other, they ask, "What difference does a piece of paper make?" Isn't the commitment what matters?

Donald Joy has pointed out that from a pastoral point of view, we should treat preceremonial sex differently from recreational sex. The couple who get carried away a week before their wedding are worlds apart from the couple who use each other's body for an evening's pleasure. We would hope to separate the couple who were using each other; we would want to bring forgiveness and healing to the couple who got carried away. Joy argues, in fact, that biblical *porneia* doesn't apply. Preceremonial sex is sin, he says, but it is a different and lesser sin—that of "defrauding one another—making the gestures of full trust without guaranteeing through social/legal protocol that such trust was indeed merited."[3]

The problem is that in actual practice (as Joy makes clear) there is seldom a clear distinction between experimental sex and preceremonial sex. Among teenagers, for example, the majority of sexually active fifteen-year-old girls say they intend to marry their partners[4]—though almost none do. Among single adults, sex is usually reserved for "serious" relationships—though most of these go nowhere. Many couples convince themselves that they are committed to each other, that marriage is around the corner. When they are in love, they believe fervently that nothing could break their commitment. However, when pressures build on them, or feelings change, they decide they are not so committed after all. Even formally engaged couples frequently break their engagements.

Private Promises and Public Celebrations
In "preceremonial sex" we can see what difference a piece of paper makes. It is a way of separating serious commitment from wishful thinking. A piece of paper—that is, a marriage ceremony—clarifies just where the couple really stands. Are they really serious about committed love? Then why not demonstrate it to the community in a formal, legal celebration?

In biblical times, when no one escaped the view of the community, a marriage ceremony wasn't needed. It was often enough of a ceremony that two people moved in together. A man who deceived a woman—or vice versa—would have to answer for his behavior. That was clearly the situation in ancient Israel, which left no record of a marriage ceremony but obviously had committed marriages. When Isaac took Rebekah into his mother's tent, his action spoke as loudly as wedding vows. From then on, he had the obligations of a husband.

The situation today is radically different. Our society is too large and impersonal to observe commitments informally. It relies on legalities. Not so long ago you could buy a car with a handshake. You can't now, and for good reason: too many people don't follow through on their commitments. They may fully intend to pay for the car, but six months later, when they are short of cash, they don't manage to pay the bill.

So we ask people, before they borrow money, to put their name on the line formally and legally. We want them to follow through on their commitments, and this is the best way we have of ensuring that they will. Not everybody needs the formality—some people actually are as good as their word—but in the interests of justice we make everybody do it. Should we take any less serious interest in seeing that people follow through on their commitments to love each other forever?

A couple needs all the support they can get. The marriage ceremony, with its celebrative vows before family, friends and God, and its legal framework, obviously does not guarantee a relationship that endures, let alone one that grows in love. But it is a support and a protection. "Preceremonial sex" would count on private promises. Experience has shown that private promises are as durable as morning dew.

Is Abstinence Possible?

Can Janis and Richard do it? If they are convinced that sex would be wrong at this time in their lives, will they be able to restrain their sexual desires?

My contact with teenagers has shown me that they can. Many do. But it is not easy, and the difficulty is not just in their biological makeup. Our society offers them almost every conceivable stimulation of sexual desire (through movies and TV), an ideology of sex that discourages abstinence, and an environment (the nearly absolute privacy of dating) that makes sex convenient and comfortable. These conditions are not inevitable. Other places and other times have organized courtship differently. (Chaperons, for example, would seem outrageous in modern times, but why so?) So long as we ask Richard and Janis to oppose all the forces of modern society singlehandedly, without help or support, we can count on a good number of failures. By no means all kids will become sexually involved. But many will.

Which brings us again to the role of rules. They cannot save, and we must be careful not to proclaim them as though they can. If we acted as though there were a gigantic difference between those who keep the rules and those who don't, between virgins and nonvirgins, we would make the rules out to be more than they are. Keeping the biblical rules does make a difference. But it does not make the difference between life and death, between saved and unsaved.

Rules are, at best, a cradle for virtue. At worst they are a substitute for genuine salvation. Whether Janis and Richard give in to temptation, or whether they manage to control their desires, they will still need to experience God's forgiveness and grace. They can never get that from the law. What they *can* get is protection from experiences that would hurt them.

11
THE ETHICS
OF DESIRE

Martin Nestor has a secret so silly, so junior-highish, it makes him squirm with embarrassment. Two weeks from today he is due to speak at the Sweetwater Christian Conference. He has a conference brochure on his desk, and occasionally he looks at it to see a thumbnail-sized portrait of the reason for his excitement: Barbara Shinar, Program Director. Small as it is, the soft-focus, backlighted photo catches the overspilling enthusiasm of Barbara's eyes.

Part of him can't see any harm in the attraction of a wonderful woman. Barbara is an exciting, spiritually alive person. Something would be wrong if he did *not* feel attracted to her.

And yet he is disturbed by his response. Martin is married and well aware of Jesus' warning that lust is equivalent to adultery. The attraction of women is so basic a part of his male makeup, however, that he can't imagine how to do away with it. What could he do? Wear blinders? Cut off all relations with Barbara? So far as Martin can see, he can't help feeling this excitement. Is it really sinful?

Yet he also senses that this desire for Barbara is undercutting his marriage. His love for his wife is supposed to exemplify Christ's love for the church, while in fact his love for his wife is overshadowed by his irrepressible desire for intimacy with Barbara. If Martin's marriage is to be a sign of the kingdom, he is going to have to do something about this infatuation. It's not just the temptation to sleep with Barbara—and Martin is enough of a realist to know that this is always a possibility, no matter how good a Christian he is. It's also that, even if he resists the temptation to cheat on his wife, he can't love her in a single-hearted way so long as he's lusting night and day after Barbara.

What to Do About Lust

In Martin's situation—and it is very common—Christian ideas about sex clash head-on with modern prescriptions. In her bestselling book *Nice Girls Do,* Irene Kassorla writes, "In order to have good sex, you *must* forget about the controls you were taught as a child concerning your genitals and your body. Adults are overly controlled children who need to be advised on how to relax, loosen up, and let go."[1] She is saying what many people believe: that our problems (in life, but particularly in sex) come from repressing our feelings.

The modern view is that desire is normal, inevitable and healthy. To stifle sexual feelings would go against nature. It is probably impossible—plug one leak and the pressures of desire will pop out somewhere else—and likely to turn you into an unnatural creature of hidden impulses and repressed sexuality. According to some, this is how truly strange sexual perversions are created. The desires that cannot surface normally express themselves in some secretive, guilt-ridden form.

Is something wrong with Martin Nestor? The wisdom of our age would say, "Of course not!" He is responding sexually to an attractive woman.

It's entirely natural. For that matter, all desire—the desire for success, for riches, for a nice car and beautiful clothes, as well as for sexual intimacy—is regarded as inevitable and innocent.

The New Testament takes a very different view. Desire (or lust, which is one translation of the Greek word for desire, *epithymia)* is sometimes seen positively, but far more often negatively. Not only did Jesus warn that sexual lust is equivalent to adultery. In the parable of the sower, "desires for other things" are like thorns that grow up and choke the plants that grow from the seed of the Word (Mark 4:19). Jesus warned that "uncleanness" comes from inside a person. "For from within, out of men's hearts, come evil thoughts, sexual immorality, theft, murder, adultery . . ." (Mark 7:21). The root of sin, he is saying, is in the "heart"—the desires and drives that form your center.

In Paul's theology, desire is the means by which the "flesh"—life alienated from God—expresses itself. The *New International Dictionary of New Testament Theology* describes it this way: "[Desire] urges man to activity. When all is said and done, it expresses the deeply rooted tendency in man to find the focus of his life in himself, to trust himself, and to love himself more than others. . . . The power of the 'old nature' (Ephesians 4:22) is seen in *epithymia* [desire]."[2]

So our desires cannot be trusted. The association of desire with evil is very common in Paul's writings (see Galatians 5:16; Ephesians 2:3; Romans 6:12; 2 Timothy 3:6; Titus 3:3). An unsaved person is a prisoner of desire. The Christian (like Martin) may be. The things they desire—women, men, houses, riches, power—may not be wrong in themselves. But so long as desires express your will to please yourself apart from God, the desires manifest sin. They are thorns growing up in the field. A thorn is a perfectly good plant by itself, but not in a place that was meant to grow wheat.

What is Martin supposed to do about Barbara? What are any of us to do with the wrongful desires that spring up like thorns in our lives? The biblical solution is never self-control or suppression alone. Paul makes it quite clear that willpower alone won't work; that leads only to a destructive internal conflict. "We know that the law is spiritual; but I am unspiritual, sold as a slave to sin. I do not understand what I do. For what I want to do I do not do, but what I hate I do. . . . What a wretched man I am! Who will rescue me from this body of death?" (Romans 7:14-15, 24).

The solution lies in a transformation through which the desires of the Spirit take over our lives. "So I say, live by the Spirit, and you will not gratify the desires of the sinful nature" (Galatians 5:16).

The Spirit provides self-control as one of its fruits (Galatians 5:22), but self-control is secondary. The word occurs fairly rarely in Scripture. It is never an end in itself, but a quality that grows naturally out of life in the Spirit. The lack of emphasis would be particularly striking in the culture to which Paul wrote. Greek philosophy gave great significance to self-control and moderation. They were the epitome of the virtuous life. One was supposed to master oneself. For Paul, however, God's Spirit was to master. The Spirit must renew our spirits with a new set of desires.

Can Sex Be Controlled?

The way Paul applies this in 1 Corinthians 7 is illuminating. Sexual desires are not necessarily evil for Paul. He wants married people to have sex together as often as either wants to, to *satisfy* desire and *prevent* sin. Similarly, for an unmarried person who lacks self-control he does not counsel prayer and fasting; he says that marriage is an appropriate solution. Paul's answer to illegitimate desire is legitimate desire—the desire for sex with a husband or wife.

However, Paul suggests another solution, preferable to him. He recommends celibacy for those who have enough self-control to manage it. (He obviously thinks many people do.) For such a person, Paul emphasizes the positive opportunity to be "concerned about the Lord's affairs— how he can please the Lord" and "to be devoted to the Lord in both body and spirit" in "undivided devotion to the Lord" (1 Corinthians 7:32-35). In other words, the desires of the Spirit for Christian worship and service would dominate such a person's life, and sexual desire would be put on the periphery.

While "just say no" strategies may sometimes be effective—we may scare people into self-control—the biblical pattern is more accurately "just say yes"—yes to some person, some ideal, some work that the Spirit has given. A young person may control his sexual desires through his greater desire for a godly marriage. A widowed or divorced person may control her desires through a greater desire for purity and single-mindedness before God.

For a Martin Nestor, cutting off relations with Barbara, or some other strategy of suppression, should be secondary. He needs to stop seeing Barbara, but that alone won't solve his problem. Martin needs to renew his desire for the things of the Spirit—including the woman whom God has united to him in marriage. Sexual desire is not in itself wrong. But then sexual desire is not, for Martin, "in itself." It is desire for a particular person—desire to have her in a way that has not been given by God. Such desire is impure, not because it is "in itself" dirty but because it focuses Martin—and perhaps Barbara as well—on purposes that are not from the Spirit. When Martin is filled with the Spirit, these desires will not seem so dominant. He will be able to put them in their place, while others rise to preeminence.

Of course, this makes it sound very easy. Anyone who has dealt with sin knows that it is not. Life in the Spirit is not religious cruise control. Life in the Spirit is warfare. It takes all that your mind and body have to give.

For example, Martin knows what renewing his marriage would require. He knows that disciplined prayer, both alone and with his wife, is needed. They may need to take a retreat, alone or together, to relearn praying together. Martin knows that Christian marriage counseling could help him and his wife face their lack of interest in each other, and reconnect through better communication. He knows that he needs to set aside time for his wife so they can talk and enjoy each other. He knows, furthermore, that the long-put-off trip to Hawaii together wouldn't hurt.

In truth, Martin could give himself all the advice he needs for renewing his life in the Spirit. His problem isn't knowing how, it's that age-old dilemma of human life: he doesn't really want to fight the battle. He's lazy, which is another way of saying that he isn't walking by the Spirit, but by his own desires.

Life in the Spirit

Contrary to modern assertions that you can't bottle up sex, it's clear that you can. It's also clear that not many cultures have tried, at least with males. Even in Christianized medieval Europe prostitution was tolerated; theologians considered it the necessary cost of keeping young men from having sex with young women. (Men seldom married before their late twenties or early thirties: the difficulties of waiting for marriage are nothing new.)

Through the Reformation and Counter Reformation, however, Europe experienced a new commitment to sexual purity. Brothels were closed down. Fornication was prosecuted in the courts. In some places, sodomy began to be attacked vigorously. Historians find that this society-wide suppression of sexuality was quite successful. Lawrence Stone comments, "Despite the late age of marriage, bastardy rates and prenuptial conception rates in the 17th Century were surprisingly low; and homosexuality was largely confined, so far as the records go, to the nobility and courtiers in the major cities." He notes the common practice of "bundling" during courtship, in which a young man and woman shared a bed for the night. Yet there was little sex, since there were few pregnancies. "Where did the libido go? . . . We do not know, and probably never will."[3]

Evidently it is possible to bottle up sexual desires. But sexual suppression is not, as I have noted, the solution offered by the Bible. There must be a transformation through the Spirit, by which a new set of desires take control.

If Martin Nestor lives by the Spirit, renewing his love for his wife and deepening his passion for God, then his desire for Barbara Shinar will almost certainly fade. That won't be the last of his temptations, though. Other desires will surface. Perhaps lust for other women will be the battlefield on which Martin fights spiritual wars all his life. Nothing in Scripture suggests that wrong desires will simply disappear as you live a Christian life.

But though Scripture never says that evil desires will disappear, it does say that they need not control your life. Desires are not the core of a person's being. They are distractions. They can lead us astray. One who walks by the Spirit, however, will not "gratify" the desires of the flesh. They will not have their way with one's life.

When people try to fight lust directly, stamping it out of their lives through willpower, they have limited success. It's like determining not to think of pink elephants; the harder you try, the more pink elephants pop into your mind. Trying so hard to control themselves, such people act like they're in straitjackets, afraid to live freely for fear they will fall into sin. This is not the kind of self-control the Spirit gives. Rather, the Spirit's self-control flows naturally and happily from a devoted life. It is not fearful, but rather determined to pursue what is right.

Whenever wrong desires threaten to lead you away from God, it is because the life of the Spirit has grown weak. Christ's life in you needs strengthening through the means of grace. It needs a wholehearted recommitment.

Walking by the Spirit means living as a Christian with all your heart. It means feeding on the means of grace: prayer, Scripture, worship, the Lord's Supper, church fellowship. It means obedience, turning away from sin. It has been my observation that Christians who do these things find lust becoming decreasingly important. Alien desires still come up, but they grow less powerful. The Spirit's desires become more hearty: experience teaches you that they lead to satisfaction. You can trust your life to Paul's promise: "Live by the Spirit, and you will not gratify the desires of the sinful nature."

12
THE SPECIAL CASE OF HOMOSEXUALITY

Christians say that God has given us a better way—that it is a blessing to be different, following God's direction. What about someone like Gary?

Until he was in high school, Gary had no label to put on his condition. He merely knew, with intense discomfort, that he was different from other boys his age. He heard them talking about girls, but girls didn't attract him. Other boys did.

In high school, during Easter break, he went with his family to the beach and fell into conversation with two young gay men. They guessed that he was oriented toward homosexuality, and they acted very friendly—almost fatherly—to him. They explained what the gay lifestyle was all about. That was the first time Gary had heard of it. He was horrified and scared, and left them hurriedly. But he could not stop thinking about what they had said. The next day he went back to try to find them, but they had gone.

Gary returned to high school more aware than ever of his secret. He was determined to keep it to himself. The news, he was sure, would be too much for his parents to take. He would face unthinkable persecution at school.

Yet Gary began to dream of a world in which he would not have to live in secret. The gay lifestyle the two men had described appealed not simply because of the possibility of sexual pleasure, but because of the possibility of living openly as what he felt he was fated to be. He dreamed of being accepted and understood, not condemned.

Christians often explain their rules against extramarital sex by saying that God wants only the best for his people, and the best is experienced in marriage. Yet this doesn't seem to apply to someone like Gary, who feels no desire for that "best." He is stirred not by the opposite sex, but by his own sex. He doesn't want marriage, and it probably wouldn't be good for him. Homosexuals who marry out of hope that marriage will "cure" them often make disastrous marriage partners. If God wants the best for everybody, isn't it a different best for people like Gary? Shouldn't their best be sex with someone whom they truly desire?

If Desire Is Natural

The gay movement is a logical result of the modern belief that desire—all desire, and particularly sexual desire—is natural, unchangeable, healthy. If that is so, then there is nothing wrong with homosexuals. They are merely different. Their desires reveal their basic makeup, just as surely as a person's desire for food reveals that he must have food or die. Homosexuals have a different set of desires; they must therefore be a different kind of people and require a different set of ethics. By modern lights it would be terrible to ask them to forgo their desires.

Yet as we have seen, Jesus did not treat desire as purely natural. Christians can never presume that a desire—any desire, whether for sex or possessions or glory—is normal and naturally good. Our "natural self" as we know it is out of kilter with its true created nature. Every desire must be tested by the Spirit.

The Spirit speaks through Scripture, and from it we learn that homosexual desires lead to sin. They were an indication to Paul, as he examined the Gentile world, that a fundamental rebellion against God undergirded that society. They had "exchanged the glory of the immortal God for images made to look like mortal man and birds and animals and reptiles," and "exchanged the truth of God for a lie." As a result, "God gave them over to shameful lusts. Even their women exchanged natural relations for unnatural ones. In the same way the men also abandoned natural relations with women and were inflamed with lust for one another" (Romans 1:22-27).

It is important to keep this in perspective. Scripture has little to say about homosexual *acts,* and apart from this passage nothing to say about homosexual *desires.* Certainly whenever homosexuality is mentioned, usually in a list of sins, it is treated in a thoroughly negative way. Since Paul regarded sexual sin as uniquely damaging (1 Corinthians 6:18), we can understand why. Yet homosexuality apparently concerned the New Testament writers (who lived close to it) less than it concerns many modern Christians.

Even in Romans 1 Paul's topic is not homosexuality. He is writing about the universality of sin, probably raising homosexuality as an issue precisely because he wants to catch pious Jews in his trap—for, having waxed eloquent on homosexual sin, he moves quickly to this sentence: "You, therefore, have no excuse, you who pass judgment on someone else, for at whatever point you judge the other, you are condemning yourself, because you who pass judgment do the same things" (Romans 2:1). He does not mean that all are homosexually involved, but that all are equally guilty of sins, which he has listed as including greed, envy, gossip, arrogance and boasting. In the same horrified tone with which pious Jews condemned homosexuals, they themselves deserved condemnation. "There is no one righteous, not even one; there is no one who understands, no one who seeks God" (Romans 3:10-11). Heterosexuals who read Romans 1 in context can find no grounds for comparing themselves favorably with homosexuals.

A New Situation

Homosexual behavior has been known in many—some say all—cultures. In very few of these cultures has it been approved; most developed civilizations have regarded homosexual behavior unfavorably, and the first laws against it were passed in Mesopotamia four thousand years ago. But rarely have societies appeared powerfully motivated to punish homosexual behavior. In some tribal societies a group of people had a special status that included homosexuality; they were not usually ordinary citizens but held a unique role in the rituals of that society, examples being transvestites and shamans.

Perhaps the most famous example of a society that did sanction homosexual behavior was classical Greece, where relations between men and young boys were admired as the highest form of love. Michel Foucault makes the point that the inevitable instability, brevity and nonreciprocity of these relationships troubled the ancient Greeks; their anxiety led them increasingly to spiritualize and desexualize the relationship.[1] Nevertheless, the claim is often made, and with some legitimacy, that the modern gay movement is rooted in the classic heritage of Plato and Aristotle.

But our situation is quite different from ancient Greece's, and indeed, different from any before in history. What is new is not homosexual behavior, or even the openness of homosexuality. What is quite new is a generation of men and women who say their desires are exclusively or primarily homosexual. They are not transvestites, nor do they have a special role in society; they are ordinary men and women.

Psychologist Stanton Jones summarizes the evidence this way: "While homosexual behavior seems to exist in all societies, the concept of homosexual orientation as a lifelong and stable pattern does not, and is in fact rare in preindustrial societies."[2] Foucault makes the interesting point that the idea of a constitutional homosexual orientation came first to doctors in the Victorian era, who shifted the discussion from sexual *actions* to sexual *perversions.* "As defined by the ancient civil or canonical codes, sodomy was a category of forbidden acts. . . . The nineteenth-century homosexual became a personage, a past, a case history, and a childhood. . . . Nothing that went into his total composition was unaffected by his sexuality. It was everywhere present in him: at the root of all his actions. . . . The sodomite had been a temporary aberration; the homosexual was now a species."[3] It is a curious irony, if Foucault is right, that the category Victorians invented to stigmatize homosexuality has now become the basis for celebrating it.

Since Victorian times we have thought of homosexuals as a category of people. Has this categorization, or some other factor of modern society (perhaps the breakdown of families), made men and women into constitutional homosexuals? Or were constitutional homosexuals always present, but unrecognized? I don't think anyone knows. In ancient Greece, where no stigma attached to homosexual behavior, every man was considered bisexual—except that the Greeks would never have invented such a term. If they had a term at all it would have been *omnisexual,* since their mindset approached sexuality from the standpoint of sensual pleasure, and you could have pleasure with any creature applying friction to your genitals.

A Misunderstanding of Romans 1
We are dealing with a new situation, nonexistent or unrecognized in biblical times: some men and women desire sexual relations only within their own gender. Since this is a new situation, does the Bible speak to it? Some homosexual apologists who want to remain within their Christian heritage claim it does not. They say the Bible in general, and Romans 1 in particular, condemns homosexual pederasty and prostitution, not loving sexual relations between consenting adults who are constitutionally homosexual. Romans 1 speaks of women and men who "exchanged" natural relations for unnatural relations. According to this interpretation,

Romans 1 must be treating heterosexuals who perversely chose to behave homosexually. It cannot deal with constitutional homosexuality at all, since true homosexuals never "exchanged" one desire for another.

This claim (made by the influential historian John Boswell, and followed by some evangelicals) is badly flawed scriptural interpretation. Richard Hays of the Yale Divinity School, in an article published in *The Journal of Religious Ethics,* writes,

> Boswell's remarks presuppose that Paul is describing some specifiable group of heterosexually-oriented individuals whose personal life pilgrimage has led them beyond heterosexual activity into promiscuous homosexual behavior. . . . Paul has no such thing in mind. He is not presenting biographical sketches of individual pagans; he is offering an apocalyptic "long view" which indicts fallen humanity as a whole. Certainly Paul does not think that each and every pagan Gentile has made a personal decision at some point in his or her individual history to renounce the God of Israel and to worship idols instead! The "exchange" of truth for a lie to which Paul refers in Romans 1:18-25 is a mythico-historical event in which the whole pagan world is implicated. . . . In the same way, the charge that these fallen humans have "exchanged natural relations for unnatural" means nothing more nor less than that human beings, created for heterosexual companionship as the Genesis story bears witness, have distorted even so basic a truth as their sexual identity by rejecting the male and female roles which are "naturally" theirs in God's created order. The charge is a corporate indictment of pagan society, not a narrative about the "rake's progress" of particular individuals. Boswell's misinterpretation of this passage shares with much of the history of Western interpretation of Paul an unfortunate tendency to suppose that Paul is primarily concerned with developing a soteriological account of the fate of individuals before God.[4]

Was Paul Correct?

Paul was indicting neither constitutional homosexuality nor heterosexual perversion, but homosexuality, period. Before modern times, the possibility of constitutional homosexuality was utterly unknown. You can't very well look in Paul's words for a distinction that was first made eighteen hundred years later. The real question is not what Paul thought of homosexuality but whether, in the light of modern knowledge, he was correct. James Nelson puts it this way: "Our ancestors-in-faith did not know what we now know about homosexuality as a psychosexual orientation, nor can we blame them for being persons of their own historical time."[5] Is homosexuality truly "against nature" when studies find it in so many different societies? when Kinsey's studies found so many Americans who practice it? Can it be "against nature" when, as we now know, many homosexuals feel that *heterosexual* behavior would go against their nature?

One might hesitate before assuming that our ancestors in faith were quite ignorant about homosexuality. Paul certainly had ample opportunity to observe it in the cities of the Mediterranean, where homosexuality was considered quite natural. Perhaps he saw things differently not because he lacked knowledge, but because he had a different point of view.

How do we go about deciding what is natural or unnatural? Modern knowledge about homosexuality comes from surveys and interviews, which establish people's experiences and feelings. But these sources are of very limited value if we share Paul's view that all humanity is constitutionally in rebellion against God. People born in sin will not necessarily feel its unnaturalness. As Jones notes, "Many behaviors judged to be sinful are cross-culturally robust; for example, crime."[6]

Paul's idea of "natural" has nothing to do with crosscultural observations or personal feelings. Hays writes, "Paul, if confronted by a study demonstrating that (say) ten percent of the population favor sexual partners of the same gender, would no doubt regard it as corroborative evidence for his proclamation that the wrath of God is being made manifest in rampant human unrighteousness."[7] Paul's assumptions regarding what is "natural" and "unnatural" are rooted in God's revelation, particularly in the Genesis account of the sexual love of Adam and Eve. This can be juxtaposed to and compared with contemporary ideas about what is natural, but neither source of revelation is able to contradict the other, because they spring from utterly different premises. In the end, one must choose which source—Scripture or contemporary experience—to trust.

Is God Cruel?

Some complain that Paul's message is cruel if applied to modern homosexuals. How can you tell a gay man that it is always wrong to act on his sexual urges? He will be condemned to a life without sexual intercourse. As John H. McNeill has argued, God would be sadistic if he created large numbers of persons homosexual and then gave them no right to sexual intimacy.

As we have seen, however, Scripture never regards desire as any kind of self-justification. On the contrary, the desires of a fallen humanity are dangerous. To live by the Spirit, people must sometimes resist their desires—or, more accurately, must allow their desires to be subordinated to the desires of the Spirit.

Suppose McNeill were referring to the common (and fundamental) desire to exert one's power over other people. Would Jesus' Sermon on the Mount be therefore sadistic? For he told people to turn the other cheek and to love their enemies. How is it that sexual desire has become the one drive that can never be contradicted? If, as McNeill writes, only a sadistic God would allow people to be born with powerful desires that are wrong to fulfill, then God is a sadist regardless of what one thinks of homosexuality. All Christians confront, in many areas, their constitutional predisposition to want what they should not have.

But God is no sadist. Sometimes he inflicts pain, but he does it from love. Scripture presents him as a God who understands our desires—understands them so well he knows they can easily lead us to death. When he contradicts our desires, it is because he wants to replace them with better desires.

What's Wrong with It?

"The Bible says" is not a very satisfying answer for people raised on

Enlightenment faith. They want a reasonable explanation of *why* the Bible says it. But this the Bible does not offer, perhaps because it does not say very much about homosexuality at all.

From what we know about the Bible's idea of sexuality, however, we can suggest some reasons that homosexuality fails to live up to the Bible's ideals. Homosexual liaisons match like with like, whereas marriage creates the diversity-in-union of male and female. Marriages can reflect the full diversity of the human community that God displays his image in. ("In the image of God he created [man]; male and female he created them"—Genesis 1:27.) Homosexual unions never can reflect such diversity.

This makes a very practical difference, too. Marriage is a sign of God's kingdom through its bond of indissolvable love. Even non-Christian marriages tend to stay together, and tend to abhor adultery. Homosexual liaisons are, by contrast, terribly fractious. Blumstein and Schwartz, in their extensive study of American couples, noted that "the only couples who adopt non-monogamy as a way of life are the gay men."

"Many gay men," they commented, "do not care if their partners are monogamous. If a gay man is monogamous, he is such a rare phenomenon, he may have difficulty making himself believed."[8] Unlike heterosexual couples, male homosexual couples who stay together become decreasingly erotic together; sex with other partners takes the balance of their erotic energy.

Female homosexual (lesbian) couples have been much less studied. They seem to be much less promiscuous than males, but their relationships are often plagued by misunderstandings and jealousies and tend toward instability, according to Blumstein and Schwartz's data.[9]

Such instability is apparently not because homosexuals are disinterested in lasting relationships. Both men and women homosexuals often idealize a stable, monogamous relationship even as they continue in promiscuity. J. R. Ackerley, describing his unsuccessful lifelong search for a permanent partner, wrote, "Though two or three hundred young men were to pass through my hands in the course of years, I did not consider myself promiscuous but monogamous; it was all a run of bad luck."[10]

Some gay advocates argue that were it not for the oppressive influence of our society, homosexual relationships would endure. Perhaps so, but that remains a highly theoretical possibility. In gay communities in San Francisco and New York, where homosexuals can live without notable persecution, enduring monogamous relationships remain extremely exceptional.

The Bible contains at least a hint of the reason for the instability of homosexual relationships, in its description of the roots of marriage: "For this reason [that is, because of the attraction of the woman] a man will leave his father and mother and be united to his wife, and they will become one flesh" (Genesis 2:24). The lasting, intimate bond we call marriage comes from a spontaneous response to the opposite sex. Could Adam have had the same surprised reaction to another man, and if he had, would it have led to a permanent bond? One can imagine that it might, but one can also imagine that it might not. Perhaps the strong bond of marriage, seen in all cultures, simply does not occur between members of the same sex.

As we have seen, this bond of love is meant to be a sign of God's kingdom. It shows forth the nature of God's love. Does homosexual love? Certainly the homosexual intimacy we know at this point does not offer the faithful, singular love that cannot and should not be broken. As with all promiscuous or unstable liaisons, it offers pleasure to the young and beautiful at the expense of the old and less attractive. It easily turns exploitative. It does not offer the sustaining grace of lasting love, and so is not an image of the love of God for his people. From a non-Christian standpoint there may be "nothing wrong with it." Homosexual relationships are not necessarily exploitative, shallow, abusive or degrading. From a Christian standpoint, though, there is not enough good in it. It does not show the glory of God's love.

The Possibility of Change
I know that this theological analysis will seem heartless to some, particularly those who feel that they are constitutionally, irremediably homo-

sexual in their desires. What are they supposed to do? They may not like the gay scene. But its sexual attraction is very powerful. So is the climate of acceptance it offers. Should they bottle up their sexuality and throw it in the sea?

I have seen too much of the misery inflicted on such people when they are simply condemned for wanting what they cannot help wanting. We must have something positive to offer them. As I have said, Christians do not deal with sinful desires primarily by suppressing them. They allow the Spirit to renew their life with a new and better set of desires.

Some people say that homosexuals can change their orientation. They would like homosexuals to exchange their wrongful desires for a Spirit-filled desire for a husband or wife. Christian groups and therapists (as well as some non-Christian groups and therapists) work with homosexuals to help them transform their desires from homosexual to heterosexual. Their work is highly controversial, with strong opinions voiced against it. Some homosexuals have gone to extraordinary lengths trying to change their desires through prayer, therapy, even electric shocks, and have been unable to change. Some speak with ferocity about the false claims they feel are made by those who advertise the possibility of change.

Others, however, say that they *have* changed. I have spoken at length to a good number of men and women who have left years in a homosexual lifestyle and are now married with children. They have impressed me as realistic and sincere. They almost always speak of the change as a gradual, difficult process, but they are quite clear that it is also thorough and deep. They don't deny that homosexuality can still tempt them, but they insist that they are not "living a lie" as married people. Rather, they say they have found a way of life that meets their needs far more profoundly than the gay life ever could. They also say that their desires have changed. They may never be quite the same as the "normal, red-blooded" heterosexual, but where in Scripture is this "normality" recommended? They claim to have found a deep sexual satisfaction with their spouses.

Stanton Jones, an academic clinical psychologist who has studied the research literature, says that the evidence is clear: "Change is possible for some. Every study done reports some successes. Some (Bieber, 1976) report about a 33% success rate for conversion to heterosexuality. Masters and Johnson reported a 50-60% cure or improvement rate. In a curious logical non sequitur, gay activists use the statistics about modest cure rates to argue that no cure is possible."[11]

Nature or Nurture?

The argument over what causes homosexuality is related to this controversy. If genes or prenatal hormones cause it, no change is presumably possible. If homosexuality is learned through social influences, it should be possible, at least in principle, to change. But research has not settled this issue. The latest reports suggest that prenatal, hormonal or genetic differences may predispose some people toward homosexual desires, but do not in themselves "fix" an individual in any particular direction. Researchers are still uncertain how much influence social experiences may have.

Whatever the cause of homosexuality, it is clear that the desire for one's own sex is deep-seated, not easily changed or removed through a simple set of procedures or one healing prayer. That is as we should expect. A person's sexual desires are very deeply a part of who he or she is.

Suppose you took a "normal" Western male and tried to transform his sexual desires, so that instead of being erotically attracted to undernourished bodies he preferred obese bodies. (Some cultures do.) What would be your success rate in making this change? Erotic attraction is difficult to explain and hard to change, no matter what it is. The erotic fascination of the nineteenth-century Chinese for tiny, maimed feet is hard for us to understand, yet it made its painful mark on hundreds of millions of women. Reformers could not simply eliminate it from selected individuals; the whole Chinese culture had to change its orientation.

Some homosexuals do change, and the judgment of Scripture on homosexuality suggests that all homosexuality must be transformed at some time in the course of salvation. The question is when: in the day of the Lord's coming, or now? The healing of diseases poses an identical question. Knowing that God wants to heal, we still do not know when he will heal a particular disease. All we can do is ask him to do it, and persist in asking, and cooperate in the attempt to heal (whether with doctors or therapists or groups dedicated to healing).

But there is another positive possibility for homosexuals: they can be celibate. For their homosexual desires they can substitute the desires of the Spirit that Paul recommends in 1 Corinthians 7: "to be devoted to the Lord in both body and spirit" as people who abstain from sexual relations.

People react to this suggestion with horror. This is a positive possibility? Sexual pleasure is treated almost as a god in our time, and certainly as a nonnegotiable right.

Yet life does not really work out that way for everybody. Most people must be celibate for a large part of their lives, and a good many for all of their lives. The average widow, for instance, will be celibate for eleven years after her husband dies. Women who are divorced will be celibate much longer. Is their life, or the lives of other celibate people, necessarily a horror?

Of course it is not. In reality, celibacy can be lived with grace and joy. I know quite well, for instance, widows who have been alone for as long as three decades after a life of active sexuality in marriage. I am sure it has not always been easy, but in their lives it is clearly gracious.

Perhaps one reason is that, unlike a homosexual's, a widow's situation is understood. She can be relatively open about her struggles without fearing that she will be ostracized. The church and community will support and encourage her in her difficulties, not stigmatize her because she has them. If Christians are ever going to provide a hopeful environment for homosexuals, the same kind of openness and support will be necessary.

We will need also to recover the high status that Christians historically, following the Bible, have given to celibacy. Celibacy is, like marriage, a sign of the kingdom. At least it may be so.

13
CELIBACY
AS A SIGN
OF THE KINGDOM

When evangelical Christians write about sex, they usually concentrate on the joys and dilemmas of marriage. The dilemmas and possibilities of single life are often ignored or treated as a secondary issue—on the level with sex for disabled people.

Yet today most people live a long period of adult life before marriage, and many never marry. Increasing divorce adds another large group to the single population. The elderly, who are growing in number, add more. (A high proportion of them have lost a spouse.) Then there is a sizable group of people whose desires are primarily homosexual. All these people call us to offer a view of sexuality that applies to singles just as much as to married people.

We naturally pity the single person, thinking of him or her as miserable and lonely, incomplete and "making the best of things." This view of single sexuality is a far cry from the New Testament's.

Equals in the Kingdom

God is in the process of redeeming all the world through his Son, and his work applies equally to the single and the married. It is a salvation that breaks into their circumstances, whatever they are, transforming them. Of course, single people experience salvation in a distinctive way. But it is not an inferior way. Our temptation ought to be, in fact, to call their way superior. (That was certainly the temptation of Paul and many of the church fathers.) For the single person's way is closer to that of Jesus, who is the pioneer of our salvation.

Imagine, if you can, patronizing Jesus as a single person. "Why haven't you ever married?" he is asked. "You seem like such a nice person. I have a cousin in Bethsaida I'd really like you to meet."

When I imagine such a ludicrous scene, I realize how Jesus transforms ordinary expectations. Matters that seem quite important become embarrassingly flimsy when we encounter him. Our dreams and ambitions, our worries and fears are held up to his light and become quite transparent. "You are worried that you might end up miserably single? Come to me, all you who are weary and heavily burdened, and I will give you rest. For my yoke is easy, and my burden is light." He offers single people a far greater joy than that which marriage can provide. He calls them, as he calls married people, to follow him.

Suppose a miserable, lonely single woman met Jesus and poured out her woes. (If Jesus came to earth in America today, I suspect he would encounter this complaint more often than the blindness and lameness he so frequently found in first-century Palestine.) What would Jesus say to her? Would he echo her mother's advice, that she ought to get out and meet some men? Perhaps. Far more certainly, he would invite her—no, *call* her—to be his disciple now, in her present condition as a single person.

Radicals and Stewards

I owe a debt to my brother, William Stafford, for helping me see that there have been two great patterns of response to Jesus' call to discipleship. One is the response of stewardship. The other is the response of radicalism. Let me describe the difference.

If you give a steward a million dollars, she will invest it wisely and honestly, and use the profit for God's kingdom. The radical will immediately give it all to the poor. The steward, if she is an accountant, will try to witness to God by being an honest and hardworking accountant. The radical may be an accountant in order to pay the rent, but his heart will be in what he does as a volunteer after work. The steward will serve on the city council; the radical will demonstrate outside the doors. The steward works with the conditions of life as she finds them; the radical seeks fundamental change. The steward sees the necessity of compromise; the radical sees the necessity of purity.

In sexuality, the steward's response is marriage. One thinks immediately of Martin Luther. He had spent most of his life as a monk, earnestly climbing rungs on the ladder to heaven. He concluded that there was no ladder: God saves us without regard to our religious efforts. That included the whole monastic affair, including celibacy. Luther had practiced celibacy, but he concluded that celibacy could only be lived by "peculiar" persons, perhaps one in a thousand. Calvin had a better-balanced view, more in accord with Scripture. But it is Luther's ideas about sexuality that have become ours.

The steward knows that the way she cares for a spouse, raises children and supports a family will often look very similar to her non-Christian neighbor's. After all, making love to your spouse, changing your baby's diapers and coaching your child's basketball team are not distinctively Christian tasks. But the Christian steward intends to do these ordinary tasks prayerfully and selflessly. She hopes to be a better parent, spouse, nurturer and provider because of her faith.

The steward's response is completely familiar to most of us, since it has totally dominated Protestantism and has come to almost equal prominence in Catholicism. In the Roman Catholic Church, the celibate priesthood seems increasingly an anachronism. A great many Western

Catholics would gladly rid themselves of it.

Isn't Jesus the Norm?

The steward assumes that marriage is the normal way to live; celibacy or singleness is a "peculiar" or unusual situation. But the radical answers this with a question: Where do we get our norms? From an observation of what is usual in the world as it exists? Or from the kingdom as it breaks into the world? Isn't Jesus our norm? Aren't we to follow in his steps?

The radical is not terribly interested in preserving and hallowing the world as it exists. He is focused on the coming kingdom. He sees the practical demands of ordinary life as an interference: he would rather serve God only. Not only Jesus but Paul is his model. In both he sees an active, dedicated life in which no practical matter—finances, family needs, political realism—is allowed to interfere with the cause of God's kingdom.

Celibacy is only one aspect of a life radically devoted to God. The radical may also, in imitation of Christ, favor a simple lifestyle, unencumbered by the responsibilities of possessions. He may eschew the right to defend himself, turning the other cheek. Often, he will give up his own individual freedom, choosing to work as part of a dedicated cadre. Thus, traditional monastic vows were "poverty, chastity and obedience."

For the radical, celibacy is not so much a sacrifice as an opportunity. He knows there will be no marriage in heaven, so he is prepared to be in that state already. Celibacy may have its difficulties, but such difficulties come when you live a dedicated, focused life.

A Brief History of Radical Discipleship

While the steward's response is very familiar to us, the radical's response seems, well, peculiar. But that has not always been so. The radical response traces its roots to Jesus, and to the requirements he made for his disciples while they were with him. (He had them leave their homes and families while they followed him.) For a thousand years it was considered the best way to follow Jesus.

The radical response came to dominate Christianity in the years after Constantine turned the Roman Empire to official Christianity. Christians, who had once been purified by martyrdom, became respectable. Something far more dangerous than persecution then invaded the church: the permissive, compromised attitudes of Rome.

Seeking a deeper purity than they could find in their churches, some men and women went out into the desert. Anthony was one of these, a wealthy landowner who left all his possessions to pursue a life of prayer. None of these early radicals had any idea of starting a movement. They were only seeking God. In doing so they caught the imagination of other Christians who were dissatisfied with the lackadaisical status quo. More and more men and women followed them into the desert to pray.

Experience taught that not everyone could lead the solitary life of an Anthony. The temptations of life alone were too great. So monasteries were established—communes of people who lived simply, shared their few possessions and kept certain standards of devotional life.

At the beginning this was a simple and informal attempt to live a thoroughly committed life. It must have shown an impressively genuine godliness; otherwise, it would not have attracted so many followers. There were other forces pushing people toward the monasteries, though. As the Roman Empire became increasingly dissolute (under a Christian veneer) and was threatened by invasion, a life of Christian stewardship seemed more and more problematic. How could one invest one's life in the here and now when civilization showed signs of imminent destruction? The monks, because they had made a radical choice outside of the status quo, were able to live independently of the ups and downs of society. Everything was changing; they stayed the same. When the Roman Empire fell apart, monastic life carried on unaffected. Nowhere else did learning and culture survive.

Monastic radicalism was not pure, of course. An antimaterial, antisex, antifemale ideology seems to have infected the monks' way of thinking from the very beginning. The temptations of wealth and position and spiritual pride came too. Over centuries, monasteries grew large, wealthy and arrogant in their assertion of superior spirituality. A monk might take a vow of poverty and then live in a palace. There was plenty of religious hypocrisy. Perhaps worst of all, monasticism developed a theory of salvation that seemed almost scientifically institutionalized. The grace of God no longer seemed necessary—or, more accurately, was simply taken for granted. This was the "ladder of angels" that Luther rejected.

Monasticism was fatally flawed. Yet I would find it strange if a response to God so appealing to centuries of Christians had nothing worthwhile in it. In fact, the radical tradition continually reasserts itself under different guises, particularly when the church grows fat or the times are unusually threatened. Dietrich Bonhoeffer, in *The Cost of Discipleship* and *Life Together,* written during the years after Hitler came to power, promoted a form of radical discipleship. During the 1960s, some radicalism came back into American Protestantism. Christian communes were launched in which all members had to share alike and live a simple life, and in which obedience to the spiritual leaders of the group was considered an essential vow of membership. In some respects, too, the modern missionary movement is radical. Missionaries are usually expected (as pastors, for example, are not) to live simply and to obey their leaders in the mission society.

Strangely, though, the value of celibacy has not reasserted itself. We have a large population of singles, yet they feel their celibacy as a punishment. Is it possible they could see it, instead, as an opportunity?

A Special Calling?
There are objections to preaching positive celibacy. Some Christians say that celibacy is a special calling, given only to a few. It cannot be forced on someone. "Involuntary celibacy" is a contradiction in terms, they say.

For example, Helmut Thielicke, writing to suggest tolerance of homosexual alliances, says that "*celibacy* cannot be used as a counter-argument, because celibacy is based upon a special calling and, moreover, is an act of free will."[1]

It is difficult to see how this claim can be justified. The only passage in Scripture that might suggest that celibacy is a special, voluntary calling would be Jesus' words in Matthew 19:11-12, where he says, in response to the disciples' shock over the indissolubility of marriage, "Not everyone can accept this word, but only those to whom it has been given. For some are eunuchs because they were born that way; others were made that way by men; and others have renounced marriage because of the kingdom of heaven. The one who can accept this should accept it."

This saying is, commentators admit, somewhat enigmatic. If Jesus were saying that celibacy must be a special calling, he would apparently identify "this word" (which only those to whom it has been given can accept) with celibacy. This is how Geoffrey Bromiley takes it: "A gift is needed if a person separated from a former spouse is to live without remarrying."[2] The trouble with this interpretation is that Jesus has not mentioned a word about life without remarriage. He has spoken about the purity of marriage, which cannot be broken for any reason. "This word" would seem to be the demand for a pure and unbreakable marriage. Who can live with the absolute demands of Christian monogamy? Only those to whom it has been given. But Jesus immediately speaks of another possibility: that of celibacy, which some have because of their birth, some because of their experiences and some because of their choice to live for the kingdom of God.

One would not want to stake too much on an interpretation of this difficult passage. But Paul's words in 1 Corinthians 7 seem crystal clear. Marriage and celibacy are equal possibilities. Paul gives no hint that marriage is normal while celibacy is an unusual "special" condition only for those who are called to it. It is, like marriage, open to all. He personally favors one choice (celibacy), but he recognizes that another might be better. He does speak of "gifts," but the implication is that either marriage or celibacy might be one's gift. "I wish that all men were as I am. But each man has his own gift from God; one has this gift, another has that" (1 Corinthians 7:7).

Paul's judgment is that a person is best off staying in the situation he or she finds himself in, single or married. These include conditions in which the person clearly had no choice. "Was a man uncircumcised when he was called? He should not be circumcised. . . . Were you a slave when you were called? Don't let it trouble you—although if you can gain your freedom, do so. . . . Now about virgins . . . I think that it is good for you to remain as you are. Are you married? Do not seek a divorce. Are you unmarried? Do not look for a wife. But if you do marry, you have not sinned" (7:18-28).

The only "special calling" Paul recognizes is the calling to be the Lord's servant. A person can answer that call in any condition—circumcised or uncircumcised, slave or free, married or single. Single people may marry if they wish—but they are equally free to stay single. The only thing that matters is living obediently before God. He calls each one of us to be his own disciple. That calling does not usually change our situation. It transforms it into a Christian vocation.

That celibacy would be entirely good for any single person—indeed, the best of all options for most—Paul obviously did not doubt. He certainly did not think he was recommending it to one in a thousand "peculiar" Corinthians.

Living like a Blind Man

How could Paul recommend a way of life that is, for most people, so miserable? Even those who recommend celibacy acknowledge its misery. For example, John White in *Eros Defiled:* "What has life to offer you if marriage and normal sexual relations will never be yours? . . . Are we implying by our question that you are worse off than other people? If so we must stop right here. You *are* worse off—*in one way.* So is a blind man or a deaf man. . . . You have a personal tragedy. . . . If you want to spend the rest of your life feeling bitter and sorry for yourself, you will have only yourself to blame for your suffering."[3]

A lot can be said for a stiff upper lip. We all certainly need one at times, and single people, oppressed by our society's glorification of sex, need one often. But is life without sex necessarily a crippled existence? Is single life at best like a blind man making do in spite of his handicap?

Very clearly, Paul could not have imagined so. He wrote of the privations he experienced—poverty, beatings, shipwrecks—but never included singleness. No doubt we are all affected by our experiences, and Paul's experiences included meeting the risen Jesus. Can anyone imagine comparing Jesus' life, single as it was, to that of a blind or deaf person? For that matter, should we pity a St. Francis, a Mother Teresa, a C. S. Lewis (celibate for nearly all his life)? No doubt they had special abilities and unusual faith to live as they did. We cannot very well require that every single person live as admirably as they. But at least they raise our hopes. Perhaps being single is not necessarily a handicap to be simply endured.

Some point out that single people—particularly single males—are prone to violence and suicide in our society. They are right: being single is often difficult, painfully so. But is the difficulty intrinsic to singleness, or is it rooted in the powerfully antisingle feelings of our society? If single people were in a supportive environment, would they have the same difficulty? For instance, did monks tend toward violence and suicide?

Others say that a single person's misery has a basis in Scripture. At the foundation of the universe, God said, "It is not good for the man to be alone" (Genesis 2:18). Adam needed a helper. God's company was no substitute.

All of Scripture must be considered, however. The New Testament introduces something beyond the Old Testament's vision. Jesus himself is the last, best evidence of what God considers good. "It is not good for the man to be alone." Was Jesus' life "not good"?

Of course it was very good. And he is not, and has never been, alone. From the beginning he was in fellowship with the Father (as Adam, and we, cannot be). He calls us to a fellowship like that with each other. Jesus made this prayer just before his death: "I pray also for those who will believe in me through their message, that all of them may be one, Father, just as you are in me and I am in you. . . . I have given them the glory that you gave me, that they may be one as we are one. . . . May they be brought to complete unity" (John 17:20-23). Anyone experiencing such oneness with other believers is not really alone any longer.

Going without sex is not, per se, gracious or beautiful. A person who cannot accept her unmarried situation will feel the "not good" of being alone. Life in the kingdom, however, can transform her situation. She is no longer alone, for she has become a member of a family. Making this real for single people should be as important for the church as its concern for strong marriages. Whether celibacy is for life or for a short period, the need is the same.

Paul's mention of slavery (1 Corinthians 7:21-23) puts all this in an interesting, and realistic, light. Paul makes it clear that no one wants to be a slave. "If you can gain your freedom, do so." We may feel the same about our sexual condition, married or single. Just as the slave ached for freedom, so a single person may ache for sexual intimacy. (A married person may, similarly, ache to be released from a partner.) But the coming of Jesus transforms ordinary judgments. "He who was a slave when he was called by the Lord is the Lord's freedman; similarly, he who was a free man when he was called is Christ's slave. You were bought at a price; do not become slaves of men." In marriage or in singleness, we can serve Christ. That is genuine freedom.

Celibacy as a Sign

The way we live as sexual creatures ought to witness that Jesus is Lord. How can celibacy witness to anything besides misery? Let Irene Kassorla once again speak for pop psychology:

> James Thurber once asked the question, "Is sex necessary?" My immediate answer is an unqualified *yes*. . . . While one could certainly argue that it is possible to survive without sex . . . or walks in the park, or music, or laughter, or the other sweet extras of living that are *not* primary biological needs . . .
> WHY SHOULD YOU?[4]

Kassorla considers an active sex life to be essential for a stable personality. "Too many women I've treated," she says, "repress their normal sexual functioning. . . . Often a closer examination of their emotional profiles reveals that these sexually sterile women have rigid and peculiar personalities, as well."[5]

Note that this is not worlds away from John White's comparison of celibacy to blindness or deafness. One may claim that a paraplegic can make the best of life within his limitations. But who would choose to be blind? And how can a disability be, in any way, a sign of the kingdom?

A Single Eye

One answer has been given repeatedly over the centuries in various religious contexts: celibate persons demonstrate self-control. By doing without sex, they demonstrate that their mind and spirit have gained control over the body's appetites. Gandhi, for instance, gave up sleeping with his wife but would take a beautiful young woman to bed with him in order to develop his self-mastery.

In Jesus and his disciples, including Paul, we find celibacy without a hint of such asceticism. They were not celibate to prove their own mastery. They were celibate because their singleness enabled them to serve God in a way that would otherwise have been impossible. They lived with a singleness of purpose, a "single eye." In Paul's words, they showed "an undivided devotion to the Lord."

This is what all radical Christianity tries to demonstrate: that everyday demands of living should not get in the way of spontaneous, unreserved obedience to Christ's command to love God and your neighbor. Someone who has given away all her property is free to serve God without worrying about a mortgage. Someone who chooses nonviolence has given up on his right to self-defense and feels freer to love his neighbor. Similarly, celibacy removes the barriers marriage puts up to spontaneous love of God and neighbor. A good spouse must give first priority to his family; he cannot easily be radical while raising children.

Consider Jesus. It is impossible to imagine a more single-minded person than he. Throughout his ministry he knew his business exactly. He could not be dissuaded from his agenda by the concerns of the crowds, the criticisms of the Pharisees or the fears and hopes of his disciples. He "set his face like a flint" as he went toward Jerusalem, to his own death.

This picture of Jesus steadfastly choosing to give his life is the greatest sign of the kingdom; everywhere that the kingdom has been preached, the cross has been used as a shorthand symbol for that single-minded self-sacrifice.

But could Jesus have made these choices if he were married and had a family to care for? Perhaps he could, but certainly not so freely. Neither could Paul have dedicated his life in the same degree to planting churches if he had needed to share his concern with a wife and family.

A single person is not necessarily a sign of the kingdom. If she is tangled in her longings and her sense of loss, she is not. But a single person can demonstrate with a remarkable clarity that she knows why she was created: to love and serve God, and him only. If that purity of heart possesses her, she makes a radical statement with her life about the kingdom.

Mother Teresa does this in our century. She is an implacable reminder to a material world that there is another kingdom. She cares for the dying, who have no value in this world, because she believes they have value in the next. It is very difficult to imagine any married person calling the world to account in quite her way.

Not many will match Mother Teresa. But in smaller and quieter ways, every single person can make the same witness. He or she can step beyond his or her own wishes and drives, to be devoted to a more driving concern. He or she can point beyond sexual desire to the cross. This will probably always be "foolishness to the Gentiles." But for those with the ears to hear and the eyes to see, Mother Teresa evokes an invisible power before which even Hollywood and Wall Street must bow.

It cannot be easy, in our society, for a lonely single person to shift his gaze from the promise of sex to the promise of God's kingdom. Even if he is willing to move in that direction, he will almost certainly feel depressed and lonely at times over what he feels he has lost. Married people feel depressed and lonely often enough too, of course, but perhaps less than single people, for they have the affirmation and support of our society.

If we feel hesitant to speak to single people about God's call to celibacy, however, we ought to go back to the New Testament and read again what Jesus promised to his disciples. They, too, were called to be witnesses of an invisible kingdom. They, too, were asked to give up family and friends, at least for a time. They were not called as disciples with promises of warmth and intimacy. They were called to be servants of Jesus. They answered. They did not regret it.

Marriage as a Sign
I have already attempted to explore how marriage may be, in two ways, a sign of the kingdom. An "easy" marriage shows the love for another that is spontaneous, joyful and naturally unselfish. Love is somehow drawn out of us, without effort. Such love points beyond our world, to a better world where love reigns.

In a "hard" marriage—and all marriages are hard at least some of the time—we discover love that endures in a sinful world, love that is passionate and simply will not let go of the beloved. Love that perseveres through pain points to something beyond our world, to a God who clings to his people passionately despite their unfaithfulness.

Perhaps it is valuable to note that in the Bible, marriage is a sign; sex is not. This stands out when you compare Christianity to other religions, such as Hinduism, in which sex is sacramental and the erotic interplay of two persons is connected closely to the relationship between God and humanity. Stories of the Hindu gods often have plainly erotic meanings, perhaps most notably in the case of Krishna and the cowgirls: As a prank he stole their clothes as they bathed in the river, and made them come to him naked, with their hands on their heads. "This story of full frontal nudity," writes Geoffrey Parrinder, "still popular in verse and painting, was given mystical interpretations of the nakedness of the soul before God." Krishna and one of the girls, Radha, became lovers, "her sexual passion and adultery in leaving her husband indicating the priority which God required in loving devotion."[6]

I raise this to bring out the distinctiveness of Christianity. Its focus is not on any sacramental meaning of sex, but on the meaning of marriage. In the Bible, the lasting and loving bond between two people signifies God's kingdom. Sex has great meaning to the partners within that bond, but in itself it reveals nothing about God.

Marriage is, as sex is not, a life of faith. We know why people have sex. They do so because they desire each other and count on pleasure. But why do people marry? Why do they promise to love and serve each other forever? No calculation of their interests can justify it. Absolute commitment tends to lead to happiness, as we have seen, but an absolute commitment can't be based on the expectation of happiness—since happiness cannot be guaranteed.

In that way, marriage points toward the cross. Why did Jesus give his life for us? No calculation of his interests could justify it. He did it as an act of faith. He trusted in God, and he loved us so much that he would give his life for us.

Where marriages are pure and loving, where they endure through the years and through all kinds of troubles, where both man and woman sacrifice for each other not because they count on a reward of happiness but because they see each other as persons of infinite value—where such marriages are known, people will see beyond the scrawny calculations that move our world. They will see another world, ruled by a sacrificial Lamb.

Which Way Is Best?
There are two kinds of signs in our sexuality. These signs are very different from each other, and in our history one has tended to dominate the other. For centuries celibacy was considered the main entrance to sexual salvation, with marriage a kind of back door for the rabble. Then, after the Reformation, marriage took over the front door and single people were sent to the back. They became peculiar, crippled people; their best hope was to endure their handicap.

Can the two signs coexist? Can we value them both? The early church did. Most of the male apostles did their work in tandem with a believing wife; Paul, Barnabas and Timothy apparently did theirs alone (1 Corinthians 9:5). Paul recommended celibacy to the Corinthians, but to the Ephesians he compared marriage to the love of Christ for the church. Jesus was celibate, yet he attended a wedding and blessed its celebration with a miracle. When Paul wrote to Timothy, he sanctioned a group of older women who had evidently taken a celibate vow, dedicating their lives to Christ's ministry (1 Timothy 5:9-14); but he recommended that younger women not take such a vow, since they tended to change their minds and wish to marry. In a very practical way he honored the possibilities and difficulties of both ways of life.

We need to do the same today. Realism is needed to face the difficulties of both marriage and celibacy—for they certainly exist. Hope is needed, too, to see the possibilities of both ways of life, especially the possibilities that come through struggle. With these two patterns of sexuality we can meet every situation, showing God's glory and pointing people toward his kingdom.

14
OUR
MINISTRY

D an Simka returned home from an evening meeting with one of his elders. The house was dark; Dan's wife was at a Bible study. Dan did not turn on any lights. He sat down on the sofa and wondered just what his ministry was accomplishing. In his hand he had the elder's scribbled letter of resignation.

The previous month, another elder had resigned, leaving a letter on Dan's desk. In it the elder had said he was separating from his wife; he did not feel fit to serve as a church leader any longer. Since then he had not been in church, nor had he returned Dan's calls. Dan had spent many hours with that couple, trying to help them. For nothing?

Now Tom. Tom was the sort of lay leader a pastor must have: reliable, unflappable. But last week Dan had discovered that Tom had been conducting an affair with a Sunday-school teacher. Tom was repentant, but Dan had insisted that he needed a period out of leadership. In a small church with only five elders, they had lost two in one month.

Dan had prided himself on teaching candidly about sex. He had often preached about problems in marriage, pulling no punches in discussing adultery and premarital sex. Yet he never knew how people really reacted. They thanked him for addressing the topic, but they didn't let him know what they were thinking.

In his vision of the church, Dan had always imagined it as an alternative society, calling people to a different allegiance and providing a wonderful shelter from the godless immorality of our age. Now he saw a different possibility—that of a church trumpeting a worn-out message about sex that few, inside or outside the church, really believed or felt able to live.

Who Are We Talking To?

In an era of sexual chaos, Christians have reason for taking an aggressive position on sexual morality. We think we know what is right, and we think the world is going to hell and would like to drag us with it. Why should we acquiesce to pornography's pollution? Why shrug our shoulders over promiscuity, as though it really were a purely private matter? We know that God's instructions are for our good, and for anyone's good. We would be very much to blame if we failed to address sex and sexuality within the ministry we carry out in the world around us.

Yet our sexual ministry does not begin with the world around us. Our ministry must begin with ourselves. We cannot be very convincing in proclaiming sexual salvation to the world if we are not experiencing it in the church. The church, as Dan Simka realized, is very much affected by the current crisis. How many pastors really feel confident that their congregation is thoroughly different from the world in its sexual patterns?

Both Old and New Testaments teach about sex with the redeemed community, not pagan society, in view. There was plenty to critique in Greco-Roman sexual practices, but the apostle Paul hardly raised the issue. He was chiefly concerned that Christians' lives reflect the glory of the gospel. Thus Paul's ultimate, exasperated plea to the Corinthians can only be addressed to believers: "Do you not know that your body is a temple of the Holy Spirit, who is in you, whom you have received from God? You are not your own; you were bought at a price. Therefore honor God with your body" (1 Corinthians 6:19-20).

Paul wanted the church to be a counterculture, showing itself distinct from its surroundings. He expected Christians to strengthen and encourage one another so that they could together reflect the ultimate counterculture, the kingdom of God.

Sexual Ministry: What We're Doing

In the past twenty years American Christians have launched a significant sexual ministry within the church. Occasional sermons have treated sex with a frankness that would have been unthinkable a generation earlier. Special seminars on sex—particularly for young people, but sometimes for married couples—have proliferated. A good number of Christian books have dealt with sexuality, on every level from serious theology to "how to." Counseling ministries have grown up, and they deal increasingly with sexual and marital problems. Some Christian counselors have even specialized in sexual therapy. Scores of ministries scattered around the country attempt to minister to the problems of homosexuals. Others encourage single people. You could still attend many churches for years without hearing a word about sex, but on the other hand, people looking for help in their sexual lives can find it, if they are willing to look.

Yet the most potent force in sexual ministry remains the most "old-fashioned"—the gospel of grace. In our world's view, each individual is lord of his life, trying to order his universe (and his sexual experiences) to please himself. The gospel utterly transforms such a view. In Christ, each individual submits to Christ's lordship; he sees that his life was made to please Christ. Further, he understands that instead of others' existing to meet his needs, he is called to serve their needs. When he sees that, he can form relationships that are durable and loving.

Church seminars on sexual technique or communication in marriage will not stop the parade of divorces, adulteries and sexual experiments as long as people in the church act on the same premises as those outside the church, searching for personal happiness at all costs. Almost all sexual immorality comes from people's efforts to find happiness. They will continue trying until they are convinced that Jesus spoke the truth in saying that one must lose one's life to find it. The most important sexual ministry remains preaching the gospel.

Within that context, three areas of ministry particularly need attention in the church: teaching our children about sex, strengthening our marriages and developing a sense of purpose for single people.

Sex Education
Every living community must pass on its beliefs to the next generation. Christians must teach their children in the faith what sex is all about. Unfortunately, practically all that we have accomplished so far is a pervasive negativism toward secular sex education.

Most school systems offer some sex education, and while its effectiveness is not observable to the casual eye, reformers urge a more comprehensive curriculum, beginning at an earlier age, and even incorporating school-based clinics that would offer condoms to sexually active teenagers. Many Christians have severe doubts about this kind of education. Can you really teach about sex without teaching values? Furthermore, is a school classroom the very best place to learn about sex? Doesn't teaching it there remove sex from the family context where it belongs, making it a part of the impersonal public sector? Can the meaning of sex and the meaning of trigonometry really be conveyed in the same manner? Finally, doesn't the distribution of condoms implicitly condone premarital sex?

Those who favor increased school sex education usually concede that parents and churches could do a better job. Yet they make a devastating counterpoint: parents and churches are not doing a better job. They are often not doing anything. Many young people get their sex education through pornography. Parents are often intimidated by the task. Some parents can only pass on their own misinformation. Few churches offer a comprehensive sex-education program. In view of this situation, Christians who "just say no"—no to every proposal for school sex education—look suspiciously like people who prefer that children remain ignorant.

Churches must help parents teach about sex. If we leave sex education strictly to parents, we know that many will fail to provide it. And what about young Christians whose parents aren't believers? If the church doesn't approve of the sex education they get from the schools, the church has a responsibility to teach them. When churches help parents to teach children about sex in an organized, comprehensive manner, no parents will be able to say, "We just never got around to it," or "I didn't know what to say." And none of our children will grow up claiming, "No one ever talked to me about sex."

What keeps parents from organizing one Saturday a year at church, when they gather with their children in the various age groups to talk together about the "facts of life" and what they mean to Christians? My suspicion is that if we organized such education, some of our non-Christian neighbors would become interested in joining us.

The Content of Christian Sex Education
Ethicist Stanley Hauerwas insists that ethical behavior is not brought about by drawing up lists of right and wrong actions. Ethical behavior is created by ethical people—people of character. Christian sex education ought to try not merely to tell the truth about sex but to form people who want to live up to the truth. There is a vast difference between teaching morals and training in godliness.

That is one reason sexual values need to be taught within the church and within the family. Within the family, sex cannot be an impersonal, abstract subject. It is taught by the person who has, by practicing it, brought a family into being. The "teacher" is looking at a "student" who owes his existence to the teacher's practice of sex. That makes the subject inescapably personal.

Any father who demonstrates love and respect for his wife, for example, is likely to raise children who appreciate loving and respectful marriages. They have seen it. They understand what it requires. And they will, if they admire their parents' marriage, be open even to the rules their parents insist are necessary. As Andrew Greeley writes, "If it is clear that the parents have obtained great enjoyment and satisfaction from their own sexual relationship, the children are perfectly willing and indeed eager to find out what their values are—how they have managed it when so many others have failed."[1]

That is one reason many parents are reluctant to teach their children, though. They haven't been angels. They feel like hypocrites offering their children morals that they didn't live up to themselves.

If they think about it, they'll realize their faults don't disqualify them. I cheated on an exam in junior high school; does that keep me from telling my children not to cheat? Of course not. In fact, it makes me all the more anxious to tell them why cheating will cheat them.

Still, this parental nervousness suggests why the whole church needs to be involved in sex education. For one thing, few Christian parents display all the Christian virtues. Ask their kids. (Paul Pearsall reports that more than half of the men and women in his sample had negative memories of the way their parents interacted.[2] I doubt this is true only of non-Christian families.)

And not all styles of healthy sexuality can be modeled by any one family: single-parent families cannot model marriage, while intact marriages cannot model a healthy single life. Children need "surrogate parents"—mothers and fathers, aunts and uncles from the family of faith to show them the many positive possibilities of sexuality. They can find such people in the church.

Besides that, young people need each other's support if they are going to live a different kind of life. Most church youth groups try (with varying success) to develop an environment of peer support and accountability. But most groups of my acquaintance keep the content mainly "spiritual." They urge each other on to daily devotions, not sexual purity. If they talk about sex at all, they do it briefly, and they do it for kids who are old enough to know all the biological facts of life already. Why such a slight, late effort? Church youth need encouragement to develop their own sexual counterculture—to support each other in a Christian lifestyle and protect each other from sexual predators.

Strengthening Marriages

In contrast to our very weak attempts to teach our children, Christians have worked to strengthen marriages. Marriage enrichment retreats and courses, barely heard of twenty years ago, have become common. Professional counseling is widely available for marriages with problems.

Yet we must do a great deal more to face the requirements of marriage in today's climate. I see this most dramatically in our nearly complete silence about adultery.

Adultery is undoubtedly the most potent destroyer of marriages. Studies indicate that adultery is extremely widespread within the church. Philip Blumstein and Pepper Schwartz, in their study of American couples, reported that

> those who attend church or synagogue regularly are much more conservative when it comes to what they believe about sex. They feel that sex and love are inseparable, they oppose "pornography," and when they are heterosexual, they do not favor equal rights for homosexuals. But at the same time, there is very little difference between religious and nonreligious people when it comes to how they act. They have the same amount of sex. They are just as satisfied. They have no more and no less conflict about sex. And they are just as traditional about the woman's right to initiate it.
>
> But perhaps the most startling finding is that religious people are as non-monogamous as anyone else. However attached people may be to religious institutions, they do not seem to be insulated from the temptations of the flesh.[3]

A *Christianity Today* survey of subscribers found that 23 percent of respondents admitted to extramarital intercourse. (This is in line with Blumstein and Schwartz's findings.) A parallel survey of pastors found that 12 percent had committed adultery while in local church ministry.

Almost one-quarter of the married people sitting in the pews of the average church have committed adultery—not last week, of course, but at some time in their married lives. It seems reasonable to assume that for that 23 percent, adultery was among the most momentous events of their lives. They may often think of it, even in church. And yet those acts are clothed in total silence. No one talks about repenting from adultery anymore. How then can people be forgiven? God does, of course, forgive, but how do sinners receive that forgiveness when there is no word of forgiveness given by their church?

At the same time, the very real virtue of the three-quarters who have been faithful goes unrecognized—for nothing is said of them either. Whatever has enabled their marriages to remain pure remains a mystery to those who need it most.

In this silence, the occasional act of church discipline—such as is inspired by the well-publicized failure of a pastor—will seem extreme to many church members. One-quarter of the average congregation has done the same thing, and one-eighth of the pastors. One unfortunate individual gets caught and punished. The church is unpracticed in discipline and in forgiveness. People respond awkwardly, and sometimes meanly. Discipline often seems to miss its goal of repentance, forgiveness and restoration.

It is probably impossible to hope that in the very near future we could develop a different atmosphere of accountability for the whole church. But at least we could look for ways to develop it in particular groups within the church—among the church leadership, for example.

We can also address the issue publicly. I am at least suggesting that pastors preach about this sin (as they have not in my generation), that teaching about repentance, forgiveness and restoration be presented regularly in every congregation, and that counseling and encouragement for troubled marriages be offered more aggressively. I do not think silence serves anyone. Adultery and other deep marital troubles are quite common in our churches. How can a realistic sexual salvation begin to operate until the realism of our troubles is uncovered and dealt with frankly and compassionately?

Singles Ministry

In recent times, Christians have been most successful at portraying the desirability of lifelong, loving marriage. Today, most people have lost interest in "alternative" marriages. Even childbearing has regained some of its traditional prominence.

But what about those who are unmarried? Among them, traditional Christian ethics have been almost entirely overwhelmed. Only a fraction of those who marry in America are virgins. "Living together" has become a mundane practice, and sexual intercourse has become extremely common—the norm, in fact—in relationships between single adults.

For the most part, these single people are not "swingers" or sexual gluttons. They want what anyone else wants: not to be alone. To many of them, sexual intimacy seems to be a fundamental human need. It certainly is a fundamental pleasure. Yet they are not married, and some never will be. Some are divorced. Some are widowed. Some are homosexuals.

Church singles groups have exploded in the last decade, trying to meet the needs of these people. There is a plainly sexual dimension: people attend because they meet people of their own age and situation. They hope to find companions, and possibly a mate. I suspect pastors sometimes denigrate the "meet and be met" function of these singles groups, but it is an important purpose. Paul himself thought celibacy was an undesirable state for some: "If they cannot control themselves, they should marry, for it is better to marry than to burn with passion" (1 Corinthians 7:9). Christians have a stake in removing barriers to marriage so that people are free to take Paul's advice.

Yet a singles group suffers when it becomes exclusively a launching pad for escape from singleness. Sometimes such groups seem to underline a non-Christian message: that sex is the end-all and be-all of life. Thus single people meet in the church instead of the singles bar, but with the same ultimate purpose—to escape from the hell of celibacy.

Must we always be embarrassed to recommend the pattern of life that our Lord, the apostle Paul and nearly all of the church fathers followed? Surely Paul's words to the Corinthians suggest something better. Surely our singles groups need to apply themselves to the task of seeing celibacy again as a gift of the Holy Spirit to the church, as a positive witness to the world, whether for a short period or an entire lifetime.

The early centuries of monasticism may help us. Christians who tried celibacy in isolation discovered that they needed the structure of communal life. They developed systems of spiritual guidance, corporate worship, shared resources and responsibility to the group. Perhaps singles groups need to become far more disciplined and directed. Nobody can doubt that a single Christian who wants to live a celibate life is going against our culture. He or she needs the strength and encouragement—and the structure—of a group that has different intentions.

What is more, the church needs such groups. If celibacy is truly a gift, we should expect single people to spend it in God's work. They have something special to offer the body of Christ. If we looked to them for singular service and leadership, we might transform the victim mentality that many singles fall into.

Our Outward Ministry

Suppose that we manage these reforms. Suppose we organize sex education for our children through the church, end the silence about sexual temptation and failure, and establish singles group that demonstrate the giftedness of celibacy. What then would be our ministry to the world outside?

It is obvious that our prime ministry to the world outside would already be in operation: we would be a living witness to a different kingdom. We would show by our lives as well as our words that there is an alternative to the sexuality of our day. We would be able to invite people into the church in such a way that the invitation offered holiness and healing.

Our chief responsibility is to be what God has called us to be, and to tell the good news of Jesus to anyone who will listen. We are not really called to preach our sexual ethics; we are called to live them. What we preach is, above all, forgiveness and the possibility of a new life.

We do have other duties, however. While we live primarily as citizens of God's kingdom, we remain citizens of earthly societies. We owe allegiance to these societies too. We have something to offer them— something that is distinctively ours as Christians.

Our society is not going to become the kingdom of God, and even if its sexual ethics became conservative they would not be truly Christian. As Walther Eichrodt wrote, the same thing done by different people is not the same thing. Lived without the grace of God and the life of the Holy Spirit, our ethics are merely the law. We are not particularly called to preach the law to our society.

We are, however, called to care for the weak and to stand up for them. In the words of Proverbs, we must "speak up for those who cannot speak for themselves" and "defend the rights of the poor and needy" (31:8-9). Who are the poor and the needy in today's sexual realm? Who gets run over by our intimacy-worshiping society? Children from broken homes. Abused children. Young pregnant women. Divorced women, cast aside as worthless. They suffer most. They deserve our activism, all we can do to strengthen families, protect the weak from sexual predators and make celibacy an honored choice again. We should fight for them in legislatures, in schools, in churches, in neighborhoods.

In so doing, we are not exactly fighting for sexual salvation. That can come only through Christ, and within the context of his salvation of their entire lives. We are fighting to protect vulnerable people from our society's evil abuse of persons.

We should remember, however, that in Jesus' kingdom, and in it alone, people will find full sexual salvation. He created us, with all our sexual potential, so that we could show his glory. We must not get bogged down in moralisms and condemnations. We believe unashamedly in absolutes, but they cannot be detached from our absolute hope in the salvation of Christ. He alone can and will make our sexual lives what they ought to be.

Notes

Chapter 1: Sexual Chaos

[1]Cited by a commentator on National Public Radio's AIDS Day, December 1992.

[2]Robert Coles and Geoffrey Stokes, *Sex and the American Teenager* (New York: Harper & Row, 1985), p. 73.

[3]*Free to Be Family* (Washington, D.C.: Family Research Council, 1992), p. 76.

[4]*American Teens Speak: Sex, Myths, TV and Birth Control—The Planned Parenthood Poll* (New York: Louis Harris and Associates, 1986), pp. 19, 7.

[5]Susan S. Larson, "Do School-Based Clinics Work?" *Family Policy* 4 (March 1991): 1.

[6]Coles and Stokes, *Sex and the American Teenager,* p. 121.

[7]*Free to Be Family,* p. 37.

[8]Coles and Stokes, *Sex and the American Teenager,* p. 133.

[9]*Free to Be Family,* p. 23.

[10]Ibid., p. 25.

Chapter 2: Marriage: A Weakened Bond

[1]Judith S. Wallerstein and Sandra Blakeslee, *Second Chances* (New York: Ticknor & Fields, 1989), p. xix.

[2]Ibid., pp. xv-xvi.

[3]Ibid., p. 299.

[4]*American Teens Speak: Sex, Myths, TV and Birth Control—The Planned Parenthood Poll* (New York: Louis Harris and Associates, 1986).

[5]Arlene Skolnick, *Embattled Paradise: The American Family in an Age of Uncertainty* (New York: Basic Books, 1991), p. 220.

[6]Archibald Hart, *Me, Myself and I* (Ann Arbor, Mich.: Servant, 1992), pp. 89-90.

Chapter 3: How We Got to Chaos

[1]Quoted in Geoffrey Parrinder, *Sex in the World's Religions* (New York: Oxford University Press, 1980), p. 226.

[2]Ibid., p. 44.

[3]Andrew M. Greeley, *Sexual Intimacy: Love and Play* (New York: Warner Books, 1988), p. 349.

Chapter 4: The Ethic of Intimacy

[1]Robert Coles and Geoffrey Stokes, *Sex and the American Teenager* (New York: Harper & Row, 1985), pp. 72, 101.

[2]Ibid., p. 85.
[3]Ibid., p. 82.
[4]Ibid., p. 101.
[5]Kathryn Burkhart, *Growing into Love: Teenagers Talk Candidly About Sex in the 1980s* (New York: Putnam, 1981).
[6]Coles and Stokes, *Sex and the American Teenager,* p. 77.
[7]Ibid., p. 78.

Chapter 5: Sexual Salvation

[1]William Stafford, unpublished manuscript.
[2]Lawrence Stone, "Sex in the West," *The New Republic,* July 8, 1985.
[3]Irene Kassorla, *Nice Girls Do: And Now You Can Too* (New York: Berkley, 1982), p. 18.
[4]Ruth Westheimer, *Dr. Ruth's Guide to Good Sex* (New York: Warner Books, 1983), p. 200.
[5]Michel Foucault, *An Introduction,* vol. 1 of *The History of Sexuality,* trans. Robert Hurley (New York: Random House, 1978), p. 78.
[6]Peter Gardella, *Innocent Ecstasy: How Christianity Gave America an Ethic of Sexual Pleasure* (New York: Oxford University Press, 1985), p. 8.
[7]C. S. Lewis, *Mere Christianity* (New York: Macmillan, 1952), p. 89.

Chapter 6: The New Salvation

[1]Irene Kassorla, *Nice Girls Do: And Now You Can Too* (New York: Berkley, 1982), pp. 33, 36-37.
[2]Ibid., p. 234.
[3]Paul Pearsall, *Super Marital Sex: Loving for Life* (New York: Doubleday, 1987), p. xvi.
[4]Alexander Lowen, *Love and Orgasm: A Revolutionary Guide to Sexual Fulfillment* (New York: Collier Books, 1965), p. 11.
[5]Shirley Gehrke Luthman, *Intimacy: The Essence of Male and Female* (San Rafael, Calif.: Mehetabel, 1972), p. 4.
[6]Ruth Westheimer, *Dr. Ruth's Guide to Good Sex* (New York: Warner Books, 1983), pp. 204-5.
[7]James B. Nelson, *Embodiment: An Approach to Sexuality and Christian Theology* (Minneapolis: Augsburg, 1979), p. 78.
[8]Ibid., p. 197.

Chapter 7: A Happy Marriage

[1]Bruno Bettelheim, *Surviving and Other Essays* (New York: Vintage Books, 1980), p. 380.
[2]Helen Singer Kaplan, "Who Are the Happiest Couples?" *Redbook,* November 1986.
[3]Augustine *The City of God* 14.
[4]Mary Stewart Van Leeuwen, "The Christian Mind and the Challenge of Gender Relations," *The Reformed Journal,* September 1987.

Chapter 8: A Hard Marriage

[1]Andrew M. Greeley, *Sexual Intimacy: Love and Play* (New York: Warner Books, 1988), pp. 116, 151.
[2]John of the Cross, *Dark Night of the Soul* (New York: Image Books, 1959).

Chapter 9: The Boundaries Around Love

[1]James B. Nelson, interview, *U.S. Catholic,* October 1986.

[2]Andrew M. Greeley, *Sexual Intimacy: Love and Play* (New York: Warner Books, 1988), p. 69.

[3]Quoted in ibid., p. v.

[4]Maggie Scarf, "The News About Infidelity," *Cosmopolitan,* April 1987.

[5]Paul Pearsall, *Super Marital Sex: Loving for Life* (New York: Doubleday, 1987), p. 24.

[6]Scarf, "The News About Infidelity."

[7]Philip Blumstein and Pepper Schwartz, *American Couples: Money, Work, Sex* (New York: Morrow, 1983), p. 298.

[8]Ibid., pp. 280, 308.

[9]Ibid., p. 261.

Chapter 10: Premarital Sex

[1]The Greek word *porneia* used to be translated as *fornication,* but is usually now rendered as *sexual immorality.* The word is general and has to be understood by its context. In most of the New Testament usages it might be translated *casual sex,* or simply *wrongful sex.*

Some would say that since Janis and Richard love each other, *porneia* doesn't apply to them. In the New Testament, they claim, *porneia* condemns prostitution, casual sex or religiously ritualized sex. It has nothing to do with the loving aims of Richard and Janis.

They miss the point, however, that the rule against *porneia* is not meant to define a set of "not-goods" but to protect something good—marriage. The out-of-bounds sex condemned as *porneia* in the New Testament amounts to all the options one might choose instead of marriage in that community. The fact that our society has invented new kinds of extramarital relationships, or that these relationships are bathed in loving emotions, would have made little difference to the apostle Paul. Clearly, to him marriage is the only right place for sex. So the church has, for nearly two thousand years, consistently understood him.

[2]Paul Pearsall, *Super Marital Sex: Loving for Life* (New York: Doubleday, 1987), pp. 65-66.

[3]Donald Joy, *Rebonding* (Waco, Tex.: Word Books, 1986).

[4]Robert Coles and Geoffrey Stokes, *Sex and the American Teenager* (New York: Harper & Row, 1985), p. 82.

Chapter 11: The Ethics of Desire

[1]Irene Kassorla, *Nice Girls Do: And Now You Can Too* (New York: Berkley, 1982), p. 87.

[2]"Desire," in *New International Dictionary of New Testament Theology,* ed. Colin Brown (Grand Rapids, Mich.: Zondervan, 1975), p. 457.

[3]Lawrence Stone, "Sex in the West," *The New Republic,* July 8, 1985.

Chapter 12: The Special Case of Homosexuality

[1]Michel Foucault, *The Use of Pleasure,* vol. 2 of *The History of Sexuality,* trans. Robert Hurley (New York: Random House, 1985), pp. 187-225.

[2]Stanton Jones, "Homosexuality, the Behavioral Sciences and the Church," unpublished lecture.

[3]Michel Foucault, *An Introduction,* vol. 1 of *The History of Sexuality,* trans. Robert Hurley (New York: Random House, 1978), p. 43.

[4]Richard B. Hays, "Relations Natural and Unnatural: A Response to John Boswell's Exegesis of Romans 1," *The Journal of Religious Ethics,* Spring 1986.

[5] James B. Nelson, *Embodiment: An Approach to Sexuality and Christian Theology* (Minneapolis: Augsburg, 1979), p. 199.

[6] Jones, "Homosexuality, the Behavioral Sciences and the Church."

[7] Hays, "Relations Natural and Unnatural."

[8] Philip Blumstein and Pepper Schwartz, *American Couples: Money, Work, Sex* (New York: Morrow, 1983), p. 269.

[9] Ibid., pp. 307-8.

[10] Unfortunately, I am unable to locate the published source of this quotation.

[11] Jones, "Homosexuality, the Behavioral Sciences and the Church."

Chapter 13: Celibacy as a Sign of the Kingdom

[1] Helmut Thielicke, *The Ethics of Sex* (New York: Harper & Row, 1964), p. 285.

[2] Geoffrey Bromiley, *God and Marriage* (Grand Rapids, Mich.: Eerdmans, 1980), p. 40.

[3] John White, *Eros Defiled: The Christian and Sexual Sin* (Downers Grove, Ill.: InterVarsity Press, 1977), p. 136.

[4] Irene Kassorla, *Nice Girls Do: And Now You Can Too* (New York: Berkley, 1982), p. 18.

[5] Ibid., p. 31.

[6] Geoffrey Parrinder, *Sex in the World's Religions* (New York: Oxford University Press, 1980), pp. 9-10.

Chapter 14: Our Ministry

[1] Andrew M. Greeley, *Sexual Intimacy: Love and Play* (New York: Warner Books, 1988), p. 137.

[2] Paul Pearsall, *Super Marital Sex: Loving for Life* (New York: Doubleday, 1987), p. 25.

[3] Philip Blumstein and Pepper Schwartz, *American Couples: Money, Work, Sex* (New York: Morrow, 1983), p. 285.

Bibliography

Annotated List of Significant Works

Allen, Diogenes. *Love: Christian Romance, Marriage, Friendship.* Cambridge, Mass.: Cowley, 1987. A thoughtful philosophical study, not technical, of different kinds of love.

Blumstein, Philip, and Pepper Schwartz. *American Couples: Money, Work, Sex.* New York: Morrow, 1983. An exhaustive sociological study.

Bromiley, Geoffrey W. *God and Marriage.* Grand Rapids, Mich.: Eerdmans, 1980. A brief, serious, conservative look at virtually all the relevant biblical texts.

Cahill, Lisa Sowle. *Between the Sexes: Foundations for a Christian Ethic of Sexuality.* Philadelphia: Fortress, 1985. This book takes a rather scattered scholarly approach, but offers some excellent insights.

Coles, Robert, and Geoffrey Stokes. *Sex and the American Teenager.* New York: Harper & Row, 1985. A sociological study.

Foucault, Michel. *The History of Sexuality.* Translated by Robert Hurley. Vol. 1, *An Introduction.* New York: Random House, 1978. A highly influential book which makes the claim that the sexual revolution is not a reversal of Victorianism, but a continuation. Not light reading.

Vol. 2, *The Use of Pleasure.* New York: Random House, 1985. An analysis of the classical Greek heritage in regard to sexuality.

Vol. 3, *The Care of the Self.* New York: Pantheon, 1986. An analysis of Greco-Roman sexuality in the period leading up to the Christian era.

Gardella, Peter. *Innocent Ecstasy: How Christianity Gave America an Ethic of Sexual Pleasure.* New York: Oxford University Press, 1985. An entertaining and informative history of sex and Christianity in America.

Gilder, George. *Men and Marriage,* rev. ed. Gretna, La.: Pelican, 1986. This much-hated book is original and thought-provoking. Some conservative Christians love Gilder because he is in favor of the traditional family and against feminism, but they should temper their enthusiasm. Approaching the relationship of male and female as an evolutionary adaptation, as Gilder does, yields a sub-Christian idea of family. Still, there is lots to learn here.

Greeley, Andrew M. *Sexual Intimacy: Love and Play.* New York: Warner Books, 1988. Greeley's idea of sexual fulfillment reminds me of thoughts I had in junior high school. Still, a number of good insights emerge through the steam.

Hays, Richard B. "Relations Natural and Unnatural: A Response to John Boswell's Exegesis of Romans 1." *The Journal of Religious Ethics,* Spring 1986. A remarkably fine essay which ought to be required for any Christian who wants to talk about the ethics of homosexuality.

Joy, Donald. *Rebonding.* Waco, Tex.: Word Books, 1986. A very interesting popular book that (along with its predecessor, *Bonding*) reinterprets biblical sexual ethics in light of anthropological studies on bonding. Joy sometimes falls into an almost biomechanical understanding of love and marriage, but in mild doses this serves as a corrective to the spiritualized understanding often current today.

Nelson, James B. *Embodiment: An Approach to Sexuality and Christian Theology.* Minneapolis: Augsburg, 1979. Well written, thoughtful, but on the whole an example of how the spirit of the age can be packaged as Christian theology. A much-quoted book.

Parrinder, Geoffrey. *Sex in the World's Religions.* New York: Oxford University Press, 1980. An excellent survey of the great religions and their teachings about sex.

Smedes, Lewis. *Sex for Christians.* Grand Rapids, Mich.: Eerdmans, 1976. Fluent, realistic and biblical. Smedes deals with the difficult ethical questions in a way that communicates to educated laypeople without sacrificing theological astuteness. There are some weak spots, especially in his section on petting, but this remains the best book available.

Stone, Lawrence. "Sex in the West." *The New Republic,* July 8, 1985. A good summary by an eminent historian of what we know about the history of sexuality in Europe and America.

Wallerstein, Judith S., and Sandra Blakeslee. *Second Chances.* New York: Ticknor & Fields, 1989. An alarming longitudinal study of the impact of divorce on families.

Other Works Consulted: Books

American Teens Speak: Sex, Myths, TV and Birth Control—The Planned Parenthood Poll. New York: Louis Harris and Associates, 1986.

Bettelheim, Bruno. *Surviving and Other Essays.* New York: Vintage Books, 1980.

Burkhart, Kathryn. *Growing into Love: Teenagers Talk Candidly About Sex in the 1980s.* New York: Putnam, 1981.

Christianity Today Marriage and Divorce Survey Report. Wheaton, Ill.: Christianity Today Inc. Research Department, 1992.

Free to Be Family. Washington, D.C.: Family Research Council, 1992.

Hart, Archibald. *Me, Myself and I.* Ann Arbor, Mich.: Servant, 1992.

Kassorla, Irene. *Nice Girls Do: And Now You Can Too.* New York: Berkley, 1982.

Luthman, Shirley Gehrke. *Intimacy: The Essence of Male and Female.* San Rafael, Calif.: Mehetabel, 1972.

Pearsall, Paul. *Super Marital Sex: Loving for Life.* New York: Doubleday, 1987.

Skolnick, Arlene. *Embattled Paradise: The American Family in an Age of Uncertainty.* New York: Basic Books, 1991.

Thielicke, Helmut. *The Ethics of Sex.* New York: Harper & Row, 1964.

Westheimer, Ruth. *Dr. Ruth's Guide to Good Sex.* New York: Warner Books, 1983.

White, John. *Eros Defiled: The Christian and Sexual Sin.* Downers Grove, Ill.: InterVarsity Press, 1977.

Other Works Consulted: Magazines and Journals

Diamond, Jared. "Everything Else You Always Wanted to Know About Sex." *Discover,* April 1985.

Farrell, Warren. "Why Men Fear Commitment." *Glamour,* August 1986.

"How Common Is Pastoral Indiscretion?" *Leadership,* Winter 1988.

Jones, Stanton L. "Homosexuality, the Behavioral Sciences and the Church." Unpublished lecture.

Kagle, Arlene. " 'I Need Space': Cracking the Intimacy Code." *Mademoiselle,* April 1988.

Kaplan, Helen Singer. "Who Are the Happiest Couples?" *Redbook,* November 1986.

Larson, Susan S. "Do School-Based Clinics Work?" *Family Policy* 4 (March 1991).

Nelson, James. Interview. *U.S. Catholic,* October 1986.

Penney, Alexandra. "Six Sex Mistakes Most Wives Make." *Ladies Home Journal,* March 1988.

Scarf, Maggie. "The News About Infidelity." *Cosmopolitan,* April 1987.

Stafford, Tim. "Great Sex: Reclaiming a Christian Sexual Ethic." *Christianity Today,* October 2, 1987.

Van Leeuwen, Mary Stewart. "The Christian Mind and the Challenge of Gender Relations." *The Reformed Journal,* September 1987.